Undertaking your Research Project:

Essential guidance for undergraduates and postgraduates

Keith Smyth, Frank Rennie, Gareth
Davies, Matt Sillars & Amy Woolvin

ISBN:1539762343
ISBN-13: 978-1539762348

CONTENTS

ACKNOWLEDGMENTS

The authors are grateful to the following colleagues who provided input or advice relating to the content of this text: Jayne Glass, Edward Graham, Jin Park, Robert McMorran, and Fiona Smart. The following colleagues also contributed to the production of this text and the companion website that accompanies it: Jacky MacMillan, Scott Connor, Mhairi Longmuir, Laurence Patterson, Errol Rivera, Susan Barrie, Lesley Murray, and Anne Chard.

Aspects of this text include adapted and updated course materials produced at the University of the Highlands and Islands. Every effort had been made to identify and acknowledge those who helped to develop this material.

Our thanks to everyone

.

1 GETTING STARTED WITH YOUR RESEARCH PROJECT

Welcome to 'Undertaking your research project: essential guidance for undergraduates and postgraduates'. This book, and the website that accompanies it, are intended to provide you with an introduction to a wide range of issues relevant to undertaking research projects at undergraduate and postgraduate education. This book is not intended to provide an exhaustive account of all the issues you will need to consider, but it does set out to introduce you to major concepts and key areas of practice which will inform your decisions about planning and scoping your research project, research design and strategies, analysis, and presenting your research.

As the title suggests, the focus is on providing guidance for 'getting started', and the definitions, pointers and advice the book offers are of the same kind the contributing authors provide to their own students when they approach their first substantial research projects – including dissertations.

Who this book is for

We hope this book will be of use to undergraduate and postgraduate students from across different subject and discipline areas, and the information and advice offered is intended to provide essential 'getting started' guidance that will apply regardless of which subject or discipline you are working within. Your own discipline area will have its own established ways of thinking about and conducting research, and we encourage you to investigate these at key points throughout this book.

What this book covers

Across the nine main chapters that follow, we will explore fundamental issues and ideas relating to what research is, including different perspectives and paradigms within which research can be framed. We will also look at beginning to scope and lay the foundations for your research project, including the importance of thinking ethically about your research. We will then explore key issues in quantitative, qualitative, and mixed methods research, and how to approach data analysis. Then, towards the conclusion of the book, we will encourage you to think about the relevance of your research, and offer practical pointers to help you get started in writing up your research.

For more detailed guidance on the writing process, including further advice on the conventions of writing up and presenting your research report, you may want to consult the sister book to this publication: 'How to write a research dissertation: Essential guidance in getting started for undergraduates and postgraduates' by two of the contributing authors to this text.

Optional activities

At the end of each chapter you will be presented with an optional activity that is designed to help you apply, or put into practice, specific aspects of the ideas and guidance that you have just been presented with. Versions of these activities are used by the authors in supporting their own students, and we encourage you to complete them to help shape your own thinking and practice.

Companion website

Our companion website features a range of additional resources, tutorials and activities relating to each chapter, which will help you to further explore key ideas or provide practical tools and advice that you can draw upon when undertaking your research.

Background reading

In addition to the resources to be found on the companion website, each chapter of this book offers a selection of references that provide very useful additional reading relating to the content of that chapter. Many of these references will help you explore key issues in further depth and detail.

Optional Activity

If you are reading this book, we are assuming that you are undertaking or about to undertake an undergraduate or postgraduate research project. A good exercise to tackle in thinking about and formulating your research is to find three research papers (published in relevant peer-reviewed journals) that are in the topic area you have chosen.

Read the papers, comparing how they gathered their

data. Take some notes on each paper, as we will explore them further in our next activity.

2 INTRODUCTION TO RESEARCH

Objectives

Our key objective within this first main chapter is to explore what we mean by research, including the different perspectives that can be adopted when thinking about research and the different research designs, strategies and methods we can choose to employ.

Key Points

Research is a structured and methodological process of investigation through which we endeavour to understand some aspect of the world around us, and the things within it.

The way in which we approach the process of research, however, should be informed and guided by: (i) what we are seeking to investigate, and (ii) what the field and practice of research offers us in terms of robust and appropriate ways to investigate that which we are interested in.

What is 'research'?

As we look around the world, we see different events, behaviours and phenomena. Our ancestors would have asked questions about these things, such as 'What makes the sun come up in the morning and sink at night?', or 'Will the sun come up again tomorrow?' We have the answers to many questions but we also generate new questions all the time. Common sense will help us answer many of our questions, but there are some things that require a deeper understanding of the world, and of the specific place an event, behaviour or phenomenon has within it. Beyond that, we want to know about causes and effects, processes, relationships, and influences. We want to understand more about the world and universe around us, the things within it, and how they work and behave.

Essentially, research is about asking and answering questions through a structured and methodological process of investigation. How we go about answering research questions, including the decisions we make about that process of investigation, is essentially the subject of this book.

Research perspectives and paradigms

There are many ways to think about and frame research; commonly described in terms of 'research paradigms'. We are going to explore different research paradigms, and understand what they are and how they are used. We will look at two different authors' views and then move to adopt a practical (and simple) position from which to move forward. The two authors we will consider are Blakie (2010) and Creswell (2009). Blakie describes research paradigms as traditions that:

have developed and mutated over more than a

thousand years, are referred to ... as research paradigms. They are the source not only of theoretical ideas but also of ontological and epistemological assumptions. While researchers may have strong commitments to particular research paradigms, I prefer to view them as possible sources of research ideas and assumptions for use where appropriate. It is possible to choose a research paradigm for a particular research project just as it is possible to make choices between research strategies to answer research questions.

(Blakie, 2010, p 96-97)

Creswell speaks not of paradigms but of 'worldviews', but acknowledges that they are also called paradigms by other writers. Thomas Kuhn was perhaps the first person to consider the concept of a 'paradigm' (Kuhn, 1962) when he discussed the nature of scientific revolution (rather than evolution) and change. Essentially, he posited the notion that science developed not in a slow and continuous manner but jumped and lurched from one held 'truth' to another. This he described as a 'paradigm shift'. Essentially, a universally held belief was rejected by the collection of evidence which necessitated the formation of a new belief system to replace the one that was rejected.

Paradigms, then, are sets of beliefs about the world upon which we build our approach to asking and answering questions. The exploration of what we understand to be 'truth' or 'knowledge' is termed epistemology. This is where science and philosophy are fundamentally intertwined.

We can consider paradigms (or worldviews) in a hierarchical manner. Firstly, epistemological assumptions inform methodological notions. These in turn inform the method (that is, the approach and means) by which the data that will help us answer our research questions will be collected.

Blakie (2010) goes on to divide research paradigms into two sections: classical research paradigms, and contemporary research paradigms.

Classical research paradigms include:

- Positivism
- Critical Rationalism
- Classical Hermeneutics
- Interpretivism

Contemporary Research Paradigms include:

- Critical Theory
- Ethnomethodology
- Social Realism
- Contemporary Hermeneutics
- Structuration Theory
- Feminism
- Complexity Theory.

As mentioned earlier, Creswell (2009) prefers 'philosophical worldviews' to 'research paradigms', and concentrates on four. These are outlined in the table below (Figure 1).

Positivism	Constructivism
• Determination • Reductionism • Empirical Observation and Measurement • Theory Verification	• Determination • Reductionism • Empirical Observation and Measurement • Theory Verification
Advocacy/Participatory	**Pragmatism**
• Political • Empowerment Issue-Orientated • Change-Orientated	• Consequences of Actions • Problem-centred • Pluralistic • Real-World Practice Orientated

Figure 1: Four Worldviews (adapted from Creswell, 2009, p.6)

The difference between the two authors' viewpoints is interesting as it illustrates that there are no universally agreed definitions and descriptions for many of the terms associated with different research paradigms. However, we shall discuss what the different perspectives broadly represent.

The Postpositivist worldview, according to Creswell, is a development of the positivist stance that there is a universal truth 'out there' waiting to be discovered, and that the scientific method is the best way to achieve this. All 'truths' are discoverable. The Postpositivist worldview has developed from the positivist in that a pragmatic approach has been adopted because when we come to study people and behaviour, we can never be really positive about our claims of 'truth' – especially when we are talking about motivation for actions reported by actors, i.e. the people active in the particular context of interest, within the world. Postpositivists take the view that 'causes probably determine outcomes' (Creswell, 2009, p.7).

This is clearly less 'positive' than the positivists' position, which would be that causes do determine actions or effects. However, and importantly, the notion of cause and effect lends itself to experimental study and thus to the quantitative forms of research we will later explore.

The second of Creswell's worldviews is Social Constructivist. This worldview holds that the 'truth' about the world in which a social actor behaves is subjectively created. In other words, we have our own subjective interpretation of the world around us, and we act within that world. What we see and understand about the world around us is true for us as actors. Beyond this, we influence the way in which others behave and vice versa. Thus the 'truth' becomes a subjective thing, interpreted by us in ways that make sense for us. Obviously, the researcher needs to understand how actors come to hold such subjective 'truths' and this is best achieved by speaking and interacting with those actors. This then, is the underpinning and basis for the qualitative forms of research explored later.

The Advocacy/Participatory worldview is the third of Creswell's worldviews and it goes beyond notions of Social Constructivism in that it uses research to justify actions to help advance the cause of marginalised individuals. It has unabashed political drivers at its heart. While mainly using qualitative techniques, it will also use quantitative and action research approaches where appropriate.

The final worldview proposed by Creswell is the Pragmatic worldview. This worldview differs from the others because it identifies specific problems and then uses research techniques to find a solution. This worldview is not associated with any one approach to research. Indeed, it utilises any technique that is appropriate for the task and as such often takes a mixed methods approach. The 'truth' as seen from the standpoint of this world view is simply 'what works at the time' (Creswell, 2009, p.11).

Research Strategies

Research strategies are the different approaches that you can take to research. Blakie (2010) distinguishes between Inductive, Deductive, Retroductive and Abductive research strategies.

Research strategies are usually determined by the way the research question itself is framed. For example, if your research question asks 'what' then you will probably be taking an inductive approach to answering the question. If your question is a 'why' question, you will then be best advised to take a deductive approach. Research strategies can also be seen as ways in which we try to comprehend the world around us. Taking each one of these in turn, inductive strategies (or approaches) move from the specific to the general whereas deductive strategies move from the general to the specific. Inductive research strategies or approaches are usually associated with qualitative research, while deductive strategies or approaches are usually associated with quantitative strategies or approaches. Inductive research is usually associated with the generation of theory whereas deductive research is associated with testing of theory (see Figure 2).

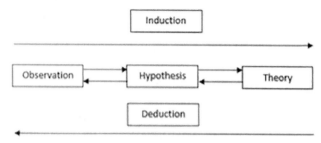

Figure 2: The Scientific Method (adapted from Gerrish and Lacey, 2010, p.132)

Retroductive and abductive strategies are often used interchangeably. The retroductive approach involves building models of a hypothesised system and then finding observations that support the existence of the hypothesised system. For example, theoretical astronomers will use mathematical models to predict the existence or behaviour of celestial objects. This can then be tested (assuming that the technology exists to perform the observations) through observation.

In the social world, abduction is the process whereby actors report their understanding of the meaning of the world they inhabit from which general descriptions can be made.

Strategies of inquiry, approaches to inquiry and research methodologies

The above terms are used interchangeably by different authors (Creswell, 2007; Mertens, 1989) but they all mean the same thing. This is an important point and one that can often serve to confuse. When trying to get to grips with research and research methods as a topic, you are often assaulted with a plethora of terms that are difficult enough to put into some kind of order. This is a problem compounded when authors then utilise different terms for the same thing.

We will look below at the distinction between quantitative, qualitative and mixed methods approaches to research, or 'research designs', again drawing upon Creswell (2009).

Quantitative research designs use two basic research strategies or approaches and these are:

Survey Research: where the researcher takes a 'snap-shot' of a situation. For example observing traffic on a certain day or, as you may already have some personal experience of, using questionnaires to gather information and opinions from participants.

Experimental Research: here the researcher will typically compare two or more groups or variables, to see if there is an observable difference between them. This involves hypothesis formation and testing, and the use of statistical techniques to interrogate and present data.

Within the qualitative research designs category, Creswell outlines five basic strategies:

Ethnography: where the researcher spends a great deal of time gathering data from a whole group (perhaps a small community, or class of schoolchildren).

Grounded Theory: where the researcher develops a theory to explain an observed action or phenomenon often situated within a specific social context.

Case Study: where the researcher examines one individual (or a 'bounded' social grouping of individuals such as a family unit or a business) in significant depth.

While this has traditionally been seen as a qualitative approach, other methods can be used to gather case study data.

Phenomenological research: this is a somewhat complex approach to research, where the researcher is interested in a phenomenon as lived and experienced by social actors. The researcher needs to be able to distance him/herself from the participants, but this is not always possible. In this sense, researchers will need to acknowledge that their own experiences may colour their interpretation of the findings but set this aside as far as possible.

Narrative Research: simply put, the researcher asks for a narrative account of some aspect of a participant's life and experiences. As we will later see, the 'narrative' can take many forms.

Within Mixed Methods research designs, there are two basic approaches:

Sequential mixed methods: where the findings from one approach are elaborated or further examined using the techniques of another. For instance, a qualitative study might reveal that for a group of participants, a certain phenomenon is important. Subsequently, a quantitative study might be used to determine exactly how this phenomenon affects the participants by comparing them to another group that is not exposed to the phenomenon.

Concurrent mixed methods: simply put, the researcher collects both quantitative and qualitative data at the same time, drawing on both to blend the data and present findings.

In Chapters 5, 6 and 7 we will explore, respectively,

quantitative, qualitative and mixed methods research in more detail. This will include further consideration of related data collection methods.

Defining key research terms

We have already acknowledged the difficulties of terminology in the area of research design and research methods, including the range of different terms that are used to refer to essentially the same thing. At this point let us stop and attempt to address this challenge. The following table outlines and defines some of the key terminology from the perspectives of three different authors we have drawn from thus far (Blakie, 2010; Creswell, 2009; and Gerrish and Lacey, 2010).

	Creswell	Blakie	Gerrish and Lacey
Research Design	Qualitative, Quantitative and Mixed Methods: A plan or proposal for research	Guide or plan for carrying out research	Qualitative, Quantitative and Mixed Methods; Consider these to be methodologies
Research Strategy (AKA: Strategies of Inquiry)	Narrative inquiry; phenomenology; ethnography; case study; grounded theory	Inductive; Deductive; Retroductive; Abductive	
Research Paradigm	Worldviews: Post-positivism;	Ontological and epistemological	A conceptual framework;

	Advocacy / Participatory; Constructivism; Pragmatism	assumptions	The culture of research communities - self-maintain and constraining (Kuhn, 1972)
Research Method	Data collection, analysis and interpretation	The procedures for selecting, collecting, organising and analysing data	The processes employed for data collection
Research Methodolog	The study and practice of research methods		See 'Design' above

Research Questions

It can be argued that the research question is simply the most important aspect of your research. Get this right and it will inform the rest of your research process, if you let it.

It is easy to ask questions. Children do this all the time and the parents among you will be familiar with the relentless 'why' question. Vygotsky (a Russian developmental psychologist) described the child as acting as a scientist trying to understand the world around them and this is a great analogy; if we flip it round – we are like children trying to understand the world around us.

Research questions, however, are a little more sophisticated than the questions children might ask. Some of the features of a good research question are:

- It must be answerable. In other words, it cannot be a question such as 'What is the meaning of life?' which cannot be answered through scientific research.

- Research questions should be justifiable from an examination of the existing research literature. There is a great phrase about science which is that all researchers 'stand on the shoulders of giants'. Think of the world-class research that is being conducted by physicists at the CERN laboratory in Europe, for example. Their work would not be possible had it not been for the work of figures such as Einstein and Newton.

- Research questions should generally fit into one of three categories: what, why and how.

There are useful ways to distinguish between different types of research question, and in the following chapter we will look at descriptive, relational and causal research questions. For now, let us consider the difference between 'what, why and how' research questions in further detail.

'What' questions are important, and are generally answered by doing qualitative research. They are essentially inductive in nature, designed to illustrate patterns.

'Why' questions are best for examining causes of something. They usually require quantitative methods and are deductive in nature. Think of them as deducing the cause of something.

The last of the usual three is the 'how' questions. These too are deductive in nature but these can also be inductive. For example, we could study a group of people alongside the external factors that might influence how their behaviour could be changed. Would a financial incentive be likely to change their behaviour? We can explore this inductively by speaking with them about the extent to which they think their behaviour might be influenced by a financial incentive. However this can also be determined using quantitative approaches such as testing two similar groups but after giving only one group a financial incentive. Changes can be measured and the ability of an intervention (in this case financial) to influence or alter the behaviour of group members could be deduced.

Often, a study will have a number of different but related research questions. This will always increase complexity but sometimes it is necessary. If you are going to use multiple research questions, then you should make sure that they are very strongly related to each other. If they are not, they should be part of a separate (but perhaps related) study. It is worth noting that research will always be more complicated than you expect, so keeping it as simple as possible is important.

See the companion website for further resources relating to the design of research questions. There is also a dedicated section on this within the sister book to this one (Rennie and Smyth, 2015).

Hypothesis

Hypothesis will be covered in further detail in Chapter 5. However we are interested in the hypothesis at this stage because the hypothesis (or hypotheses) is usually developed during the initial stages of designing your research. A hypothesis is developed when we use a deductive approach and especially when we are comparing two different things. Essentially, the hypothesis is the prediction that there will be no difference between two groups and the measurements of them after some sort of experimental manipulation. If a difference is found, then it can be concluded that this was the result of the experimental manipulation and the hypothesis will be rejected in favour of an alternative or experimental hypothesis. Non-experimental research does not require a hypothesis and, indeed, it would be inappropriate to use a hypothesis in anything other than an experiment.

Positioning your own research

No research exists in isolation, and as alluded to previously, it is important to understand what is already known about a topic before embarking on a piece of research. This applies to any formal piece of research, regardless of the level of the research or size of the project.

Depending on where you are at with your own research, you will no doubt have done some initial reading around your topic and may even have begun conducting and writing up a literature review. This is an important task, and will help inform and refine your research as well as enable you to position your own research against the work that has come before it. You will then be able to make justifiable decisions about your own research question(s), where you are addressing a need for further research (which might include the need for research on a specific topic in a particular context), and which data collection and analysis methods you will employ.

Do not be afraid to be critical of previous research. This is part of the academic process. Findings from your research may contradict other findings and this is fine. However, in order to make a robust defence of your research, you need to be confident in your research methods and methodology. Equally, when you are critical of other studies, you may well identify shortcomings in the method or methodology of that study. In this sense, you are stating where you think your research fits in to the wider body of knowledge and thus defending that position. You are also enabling yourself to understand – and communicate to your tutors and peers – which research tradition or 'research paradigm' your own research belongs to, or most closely aligns with.

Background Reading

Blakie N. (2010) Designing social research (2nd Edition). Cambridge: Polity.

Creswell, J.W. (2007) Qualitative inquiry and research design (2nd Edition). Sage.

Creswell, J.W. (2009) Research design: Qualitative, quantitative, and mixed methods approaches, 3rd Edition. London: Sage.

Gerrish K. and Lacey A. (2010) The research process in

nursing (6th Edition). Oxford: Wiley-Blackwell.

Guba, E.G. (1990) The alternative paradigm dialogue. In E.G. Guba (Ed.) The paradigm dialogue. California: Sage, pp. 17-30.

Hycner, R. H. (1999). Some guidelines for the phenomenological analysis of interview data. In A. Bryman & R. G. Burgess (Eds.) Qualitative research (Vol. 3). London: Sage, pp. 143-164.

Kuhn, T.S. (1962) The structure of scientific revolutions. Chicago: University of Chicago Press.

Marshall, C. and Rossman, G.B. (1999) Designing qualitative research (3rd Edition). Sage.

Rennie, F. and Smyth, K. (2015) How to write a research dissertation: Essential guidance in getting started for undergraduates and postgraduates. eTIPS: University of the Highlands and Islands and Edinburgh Napier University.

3 LAYING THE FOUNDATIONS FOR YOUR PROJECT

Objectives

The objective of this short chapter is to help you gain an understanding of how to begin scoping your research, including key considerations in forming your research and identifying sources of data.

Key Points

It should go without saying that it is impossible to investigate a specific research problem unless that problem is at first articulated and clarified, but you might be amazed at how many novice researchers try to do just that! Commonly, a research project will begin with an interest in a general subject area, or an identified topic. This will lead to the formulation of a working title covering the subject area, such as 'the geology of the Isle of Lewis' or 'the mediaeval history of Tain'. This is enough information to allow the researcher to begin to become familiar with the broad area of the discipline, and perhaps give an insight into some details of a sub-topic, but this is not a research question in itself. To structure a research project – that is, to conduct a systematic investigation of a topic in order to gain new insights – the researcher needs to either identify a particular research question, or propose a hypothesis to be tested.

The results from these processes are the focus of the individual research project. We will deal with both of these activities further on, but there are several steps which the researcher can usefully take before she or he reaches this stage..

Identifying your focus

One of the key drivers of research at any level is simple personal curiosity; 'what happens if I do this?' or 'what actually happened in that situation?' is often the starting point for a more complex investigation. Different disciplines approach the next stage differently, for example a physical scientist might construct a laboratory experiment, while a social scientist might start with a detailed bibliographical survey of what is already known. Either way, the researcher needs to build on their previous knowledge and experience by acquiring a detailed knowledge of the general area to be investigated. In identifying what is already known about the subject area, it should then become easier to identify what is less well-known, and therefore what are potentially fruitful areas for a future research study.

With most researchers, whether novice or more experienced, the identification of this focus will be greatly assisted by discussing the research potential with peers and with supervisors. Just because something is unknown to you does not mean that it is not well-known to the rest of the academic community. Normally, several (perhaps many) less well-known areas will be identified, and these can be clustered together into related areas which can be jointly investigated. The specific focus might change over the duration of the research project, but the general focus should remain broadly similar.

With large-scale research projects lasting several years, such as a PhD, the focus of the research will start with a broad base, and become sharper and more clearly focussed during the ongoing research process, to finally provide an 'answer' or 'an interpretation', or simply 'a summation of what is now known'. Do not be surprised or worried if, as a new or less experienced researcher, you find it difficult to focus sharply on a clearly defined research topic at the outset. Enthusiasm for the topic will go a long way, and careful attention to the details of the formulation of the research problem and subsequent data collection, which we will deal with next, will usually help to provide a useful framework to advance the investigation one step at a time.

Problem formation

Stemming from the initial personal interest in the general subject area of the research, the next step is to identify a particular problem or issue to investigate in more depth. The two common methods for further investigation are: (i) to pose a research question, then seek to answer this question, or (ii) to propose a particular hypothesis which is then tested. Both methods are valid, and different academic disciplines will normally favour one approach or the other.

An initial research question might simply be piece of 'blue sky' thinking (what happens if....?) but it needs to be clearly worded so that it is possible to get an answer. A research hypothesis is more positivist than interrogative. A hypothesis might propose 'If I do X, or think of X in this way, then Y outcome will result'. The research process will then test if Y is actually the outcome, and seek a theory of cause and effect to explain this.

There are several different types of research question, such as:

Descriptive: a straightforward description of the problem (e.g. 'How many species of fish are there in Loch Ness?')

Relational: making comparisons between one or more variables (e.g. 'What proportion of Honours degree students go on to do a Master's degree?')

Causal: which attempts to determine if one or more independent variables cause variation in one or more dependent variables (e.g. 'What are the main factors of student induction which affect the quality of student performance in their subsequent degree?')

Whichever type is chosen will depend upon the combination of what is already known about the subject area, what the study seeks to discover, and what are the (known) sources of primary data which might be gathered to provide evidence. A good tip is to write down (in a research notebook or a file on your computer) the questions which come to mind as the previous research literature is reviewed. This will likely lead to a long list of questions, some easy, some hard; some of which will be answered during the course of the research, others which will remain unanswered. Building up this list of questions should help to identify clusters of common issues, and by prioritising these, to formulate an over-arching question which captures the heart of the research problem.

A number of crucial factors will influence the development of the research question, such as:

- what can be effectively studied within the time-frame and financial constraints of the study

- the ability to make an original contribution to knowledge (however small)

- the ethical requirements of the subject discipline (mentioned in chapter four)

- any anticipated relationship to established theories and practices of the subject area

During the evolution of a long research project, the main research question is likely to remain constant, but many of the sub-questions might change in priority, or indeed be discarded in favour of more promising or more interesting areas of study.

A fundamental influence on the prioritisation of the subsidiary research questions will be the ability to match the questions with potential sources of relevant information which can be gathered systematically using appropriate research methods.

Identifying your subjects and sources

As the researcher begins to articulate relevant research questions, the next stage is to identify what sort of information will be necessary in order to answer these questions, (e.g. participant's views, official statistics etc.) and possible sources of such information.

An obvious initial source of information will come from a review of the previously published academic literature. Not only will this indicate which aspects of the research problem are known, or have already been explored, but it will provide details on the research methods of previous studies and the types of resources which have been used. It may even be discovered that a very similar study has already been described in detail, allowing a new research project to replicate this study and compare with the previous results in order to substantiate or challenge those.

Identifying the sort of information which will be required to answer the research question needs to take place in parallel with deciding on the research methods which will be used to gather the information. For example, if the research question wishes to determine the effectiveness of a piece of equipment, or a new piece of software, then it is likely that the required information could be provided by the people who use that item.

A decision then needs to be taken on the best way to gather the information from the users – it could be via a series of in-depth interviews, or if a larger number of users is required and the information can be categorised simply, a questionnaire might be more appropriate. This would lead to a number of logistical considerations, such as how will the users be identified (e.g. all users in a particular firm or in a certain region of the country; or is a randomly selected population more appropriate?). Another immediate consideration will be how to gather this information from the users – if it is by a questionnaire, should this be an online questionnaire or a paper-based format? Both types will have different benefits and disadvantages.

From another perspective, a research question which relies on historical data may have a completely different set of potential sources and methods of gathering information, if for no other reason than it is of course impossible to interview people from a previous century. In each case, the research questions and sub-questions will still need to be matched with potential sources of information, and decisions will still need to be made on how these sources can be identified and harvested. An example might be the need to search the archives of a particular library, or to re-examine a certain type of artefact in every museum in the country.

The potential sources of information might be easily identified, but actually being able to gather the relevant information in sufficient quantity and reliable quality may prove difficult or impossible. There may also be good ethical reasons which prevent detailed information being gathered. All these different aspects of the research project – what research question is being asked; where the potential data sources can be located that will help to answer this question; what methods are needed to interrogate these sources – need to be carefully planned to consider a diversity of situations.

Constructing a research plan

There are several 'golden rules' to bear in mind when starting to prepare a plan for a research project, no matter if the project is large or small, long-term or only a short duration.

Firstly, the initial research plan is only an indication of how the researcher would like to see the project progress to a successful conclusion. Once the data-gathering stage is in operation, there are many reasons why the plan might need to be modified to improve the process (e.g. people might not respond to requests for information, or may return too much, or too little detail). For this reason, it is a good idea to have given some thought to a 'plan B' if things go wrong. Can the information be obtained from another source? Can different information be used to provide an answer to the same question? Would different research methods prove more effective?

Before starting the research project, print out the main research question and hang it somewhere prominent where it catches the eye and reminds the researcher(s) every day of the reason for doing this research. There are many potential distractions, but this one simple act may help to retain your original focus.

The research plan should not only indicate the general strategy for data collection and the methods chosen to gather the data, it should also indicate why these methods have been chosen over all the other possible research methods potentially available to the researcher. To provide additional guidance, an approximate time-scale for each stage of the research project needs to be drafted – perhaps through the construction of a simple Gantt chart – and key milestones need to be identified. Be realistic in this assessment of the time that may be required. Although this time-line may only be for your own guidance rather than hard-and-fast, externally-imposed deadlines, it is a good discipline to adhere to.

A second 'golden rule' is not to over-complicate the research process. A simple, elegant 'solution' can be much more satisfying than a convoluted one which depends upon assumptions, caveats, and wishful thinking!

It is a good idea to pilot the chosen data-gathering processes before embarking on the main phase of the data-gathering. The pilot is normally conducted with a small sample size and is used to ensure that the questionnaire, or the interview schedule, or the laboratory experiment runs smoothly and clearly. If the different research sub-questions are open to different interpretations, then people will certainly interpret them differently, and your results will be ambiguous at best and unusable at worst. The pilot phase does not need to involve a lot of extra work, but if properly done it can save a lot of work at a later stage.

As a general rule, for all levels of research engagement, it is better to be less ambitious with the research question and more robust with the methodology and research methods than it is to be over-ambitious and less robust with the methods. The former can lead to small advances in the subject area but the results can be relied upon with certainty, whereas the latter produces results which may appear dramatic, but are undermined by the lack of clarity, precision, and reliability required. A good research plan can help prevent this

Optional Activity

Find out about and explore a tool called Tom's Planner which we have linked to from the companion website. Use Tom's Planner to create an initial Gantt chart to act as a plan for your research project. You may want to refine this Gantt chart as you work through the other chapters of this book, and/or as you begin to scope out your research project in more detail.

Background Reading

Blaxter, L., Hughes, C., and Tight, M. (2010) How to research (4th Edition). The Open University Press.

Bryman, A. (2012) Social research methods (4th Edition) Oxford University Press.

Murray, R. (2002) How to write a thesis. Open University Press.

SMYTH, RENNIE, DAVIES, SILLARS & WOOLVIN

4 ETHICAL CONSIDERATIONS

Objectives

The main objective of this chapter is to outline the purpose of research ethics, and how ethical considerations can and should influence how you plan and conduct your research.

Key Points

When the subject of ethical behaviour with respect to research is raised, there are only two certainties. The first is that there are ethical considerations embedded in all research projects. The ethical issues may be very different, and some areas of research require higher levels of ethical assurances than others, but the requirement to observe appropriate ethical behaviour is incumbent on all researchers. It is worth noting here that ethical behaviour is socially constructed, and is not absolute, so it will vary with time and context; e.g. when working with children or vulnerable adults.

The second certainty is that the onus is upon the researcher(s) to demonstrate that their conduct is within the law and will not cause harm to anyone as a result of any actions pertaining to the research. The cardinal principle to be applied is to ensure respect for human dignity.

Thinking ethically

The above may sound a bit extreme, and perhaps a bit frightening at first, but when we consider the wide scope of the phrase 'research activities' we can hopefully demystify the trepidation around ethical considerations and academic research.

Furthermore, in exploring the ethical implications of research, it can help to inform and self-critique how you approach the research, and those you wish to involve in that research. Fundamental considerations of research ethics include the need to demonstrate in the research design the free and informed consent of the participants, veracity in participant exchanges, respect for vulnerable persons, privacy and confidentiality, justice and inclusiveness, and the balance between the potential harms and benefits which may occur to all of those involved in the study.

To begin with, there are some areas of research activities which are more stringently scrutinised in order to ensure that high levels of ethical behaviour are being observed. Disciplines such as medicine, and all related subjects which require access to patients, to medical records, or which have any involvement with drugs, medications, and patient treatments, come high on the priority list for ethical scrutiny. This is because there may be a real risk of causing physical or mental harm, even death, to individuals associated with the research. The harm may be accidental, such as stigmatising a patient by revealing some aspect(s) of their personal medical history, but for these reasons there are very careful controls over all research related to human health. In the UK all universities adhere to the National Health Service codes and ethical approval procedures. This level of ethical clearance for research is very robust, and can be a lengthy process, so all students involved in such activity will need to seek expert guidance from their research supervisors.

Another high-scrutiny area is any research activity working with animals. For many of the same reasons as human health, any research with live animals has the possibility of causing distress or injury, and to avoid this the research activities need to be clearly designed and carefully regulated. In a similar way, any research activities which place the researcher(s) in high-risk situations – such as extreme natural environments, delicate industrial locations, or sensitive locations, such as war-zones or other areas which might be personally dangerous, need to be given high levels of consideration before the research is attempted.

Away from such high-priority areas, there may be less extreme repercussions for any lapse in ethical integrity, but the results can still be serious. Aside from straightforward moral issues, such as not stealing, spying, or otherwise illegally acquiring research data, it is expected that researchers will not bribe, buy, or use underhand methods to conduct their research.

Ensuring anonymity

While the vast majority of research projects do not need to deal with such dramatic situations, there is still a requirement to reflect upon the ethical implications of any research work. A common issue to consider is to ensure that any informants who share their views or provide evidence for the study can remain anonymous. There are two main reasons for this. Firstly, because the informants may be targeted or abused by others for sharing information that other people dislike, or would prefer not to be made known. Secondly, the informants might not be entirely open and honest with the researcher(s) if they suspect that their views are going to be publicly attributed, or that other people might subsequently give them a hard time for talking to a researcher. For these reasons it is vital that many, if not all, research participants are listed anonymously – usually this is simply noted as 'Respondent 7' or by using fictional names, although the researchers should keep a separate list of respondent identities which is for private authentication only. One strategy may also be to anonymise where the research has been conducted. This could involve describing the characteristics of the area but giving it a fictional name providing a further level of anonymity to the participants.

This need to protect data sources extends more widely than simply re-naming the area and/or people who have been interviewed for the study, it includes the need to hold the data (and identities) securely and safely. In most circumstances this is easily done by not leaving data in public view, lying in unlocked drawers, or on computer devices without password access. For many research initiatives, however, the funders will demand that the funding application contains details of what data is to be gathered, how will it be stored, where will it be stored, for how long, and who will have access? For large structured research projects especially, there is a need to think about what will happen to the data after the project is completed and staff move on. There is an obligation on the university to ensure that the research data continues to be safe, but can be made available to any researchers in future, should the need arise.

Informed consent

Following the same line of thought, it is necessary to ensure that any participants who are engaged with the study are fully aware what the study is about, who the researchers are, and what is planned to be done with the research data. Normally this can be covered by a concise written introduction which can be given to participants to keep at the start of an interview and explained to the participants before the interview commences.

Participants need to be aware that they can withdraw from the research study at any time without prejudice or any subsequent unpleasant consequences. Researchers need to be aware that while the withdrawal of participants during the study can make gathering data more difficult, it is another good reason why researchers need to be open, honest, and up-front with participants at the very start of the research. Requesting participants to sign an informed consent form should be standard practice to ensure that participants have understood what the research is about and what their involvement entails. It also allows researchers to keep a record of their ethical practices should anyone ask.

The increasing incorporation of digital technology into the education sector both simplifies and complicates the nature of research activities. On one hand, there are lots of new applications which can assist data collection, such as smartphones with digital recording software, or online fora to network discussions (and results) beyond the immediate campus. On the other hand, while the utilisation of convenient digital communication tools such as Facebook, Twitter, Skype, or SurveyMonkey can allow access to a greater number of participants, the third-party nature of their ownership means that these communications are never entirely private, as most social media services reserve the right to read users' correspondence. This has obvious implications for data security and participant anonymity.

While not every research project includes one-to-one interviews or focus groups with human participants, this is the area of common concern, and ethical considerations need to be integral to the research-planning process, whether this refers to online surveys or laboratory experiments. Research ethics approval is solely about ensuring that no harm is done – intentionally or accidentally – and this includes not just physical or mental harm, but also harm to reputations (of individuals, organisations, the university) and about demonstrating a professional code of standards for those who engage in research.

Seeking ethical approval

Normally, the issue of ethical approval for research is considered at a very early stage in the research project. Once the researchers have familiarised themselves with the academic literature and have begun to identify the types of data that will be needed to begin to answer the research question, it will become clearer what sort of data-gathering methods will need to be employed.

When there is an understanding of the proposed research methods and potential sources of data, there should be an application for ethical approval for the research before anything else is done. This is crucial, because most institutions will prohibit the use of any data gathered before ethical approval has been granted, and may even take further action against those who have proceeded without the proper authorisation. For this reason, universities have a formal Research Ethics Committee to administer the institutional process for the ethical approval of research projects by staff and students, so seek guidance there if required.

It makes sense to consider the ethical requirements right from the start of the research design process, and as noted earlier, this may have slightly different requirements in different disciplines. Many professional associations and public funders of research have detailed explanations of the required procedures for research ethics in their subject areas, and these are frequently hosted on their websites. Although many of the ethical requirements for the safe and efficient conduct of research appear to be common-sense, there are also many pit-traps for the unwary, and the level of detailed consideration required should not be minimised. If in doubt, play safe, and always discuss the issues in depth with a research supervisor before you begin to collect data for your project.

It is important to remember that ethical considerations do not end once the ethical approval form has been submitted and approved. There are some who argue for more 'participatory ethics' (see for example Manzo and Brightbill, 2007). This calls for ethical considerations to be embedded within the research process, for the researcher to be more reflective of how they are conducting their research and to ensure more collaboration between researcher and participants in response to ethical issues. Questions around the ethics of the research may only arise once the researcher is out in the field, so responding and making decisions about these ethically may also be necessary.

The ethical considerations of research will vary between each research project. Some research will have clearly defined ethical questions from the outset, such as those involving vulnerable persons, animals or research being undertaken in high-risk areas. For other projects, the considerations may be less obvious or seem easier to address. No matter which end of the spectrum is being considered, it is important to put strategies in place to help researchers to answer ethical questions or fulfil ethical requirements, such as participant anonymity and confidentiality. Institutions will require ethical approval to be gained before any research is undertaken.

Finally, it is good practice to be reflective of your research activity and to bear in mind the ethical implications which you may encounter while conducting your research, whether at the design phase, in the field, or writing up the research documentation.

Optional Activity

Locate your own institution's research ethic guidelines (they should be available through your institution's Research Ethics Committee or similar). Once you have located them, review the guidelines carefully to consider the potential implications of them for your own project.

Background Reading

Bryman, A. (2012) Social research methods (4th Edition) Oxford University Press.

Manzo, L.C. and Brightbill, N. (2007) Towards a participatory ethics. In S. Kindon, R. Pain, & M. Kesby, (Eds.) Participatory action research approaches and methods: Connecting people, participation and place. London: Routledge, pp. 33–40.

5 QUANTITATIVE RESEARCH METHODS

Objectives

Our objectives within this chapter are many, and in our exploration of key concepts and considerations relating to quantitative research we will: introduce the concept of quantitative analysis; consider the planning cycle; differentiate between primary and secondary sources of data; and introduce sampling approaches and statistical tests.

Key Points

Fundamentally, quantitative research methods are about objective measurement. This simply means to use numbers to explain our research findings. Our research may involve questionnaires or surveys, investigating opinion using scales, or be more experimental using tests which measure performance or ability. Regardless, quantitative research uses numerical data to describe findings.

As we began to explore in Chapter 2, some quantitative studies may be descriptive in nature and set out to show differences between groups of people which may exist, for example, in terms of their opinions or attitudes. We may be able to demonstrate that differences between groups are significant or meaningful, and also demonstrate how a population may be broken up into clusters of people with different attitudes and opinions. In experimental studies, often used in psychology, quantitative methods are used to find out if there is a cause and effect relationship between variables which can be measured by using numerical data.

By using both descriptive and inferential statistics we can demonstrate that this cause and effect relationship is genuine and not the result of a chance occurrence, or the result of another unknown variable. Consequently, good quantitative research is 'controlled' sufficiently to ensure that the influence of extraneous or confounding factors is reduced to a minimum, whilst at the same time the study is not so artificial that it lacks any real world meaning. Although we try to establish beyond doubt that a particular variable 'caused' an 'effect', we must remember that statistics are based on probability – so we can only very rarely state that we have 'proven' cause and effect. However, through replication (the repeating of an experiment) we can demonstrate that an effect is robust.

As also noted in Chapter 2, research design has a great many technical terms associated with it and quantitative research is probably one of the most complex in this respect. Therefore, we have included a glossary at the end of the chapter which defines many of the terms you will encounter.

The outcome of any research method is the ability to tell the 'story' of the data. Within quantitative research, this means to translate the statistics and numbers into a narrative which explains how the research question has been addressed. To be able to do this with confidence we need to transfer the ideas (or phenomena) in the research question into something that is measurable.

Planning quantitative research

A number of phases are involved in the quantitative research process and you will find that although there is a linear progression towards an end goal, planning is not a simple unidirectional process and is iterative as we cycle through certain stages (See Figure 3 on following page).

This process divides neatly into the Planning and Execution stages.

Decisions made in early stages often have to be modified to enable later stages to contribute more effectively to the final interpretation of the findings. A key consideration must be the test you use at the end to analyse the data, which is the final stage in the planning process.

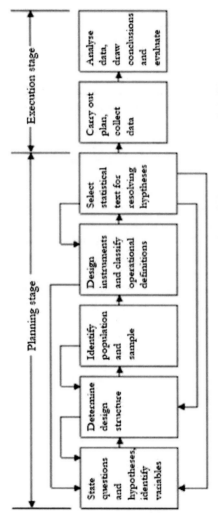

Figure 3: Stages of designing in carrying out quantitative research (Black, 1999)

Primary and secondary sources of data

Quantitative research methods use both primary and secondary sources. Emphasis is often placed on data which your own research generates – i.e. primary data – but we also consider here secondary analysis which uses existing datasets.

Primary Sources

When thinking about research, most people consider primary sources first of all. This is simply defined as the evidence the research generates directly as part of the study. This may be in the form of questionnaires, surveys or experimental data. It is unique to the study and will not be found anywhere else. However, there are other forms of data which are available to researchers and which are often used. Today, large datasets are often held by governments and other agencies and are made openly available to the research community. Research using this kind of data would be known as secondary source research and would involve secondary analysis of previously gathered data.

Secondary Analysis

Secondary analysis is defined as 'any further analysis of an existing dataset which presents interpretation, conclusions or knowledge additional to or different from those presented in first report on the inquiry as a whole and its main results' (Hakim, 1987).

There are a surprising number of existing data sets on a whole range of topics available to researchers. These range from census information to more detailed data sets on highly specific topics. Academic research is often funded by public bodies and there has been a recent move towards ensuring that publicly funded research has open access to any data gathered. Although there are ethical issues and access issues to be considered, this sea change will mean that more and more secondary sources will become available over time. The use of secondary data sets will therefore present increasing opportunities for new research and new research questions.

Examples of secondary data types and sources include:

- Population censuses, e.g. the UK census

- Continuous and regular surveys, e.g. General Household surveys

- Cohort studies, e.g. National Childhood Development Survey

- Datasets from administrative or public records, e.g. surveys done by local councils or public organisations

- Pooled data in discipline specific repositories which include natural and physical sciences.

You may want to consult the companion website for this book, where you can access and explore various examples of publicly available datasets including census and other forms of data.

Advantages and disadvantages of secondary analysis

Some of the advantages of secondary analysis are as follows:

- Pragmatically, using secondary data can save a significant amount of cost and time that would have been spent on data collection.

- Methodologically, secondary data available from the public data archives are likely to be drawn from the extensive population by professional researchers.

- Theoretically, the datasets you are using are fully explored, providing new insights as a result of being examined using different variables or analysed by different methods.

- Increased possibility of analysing data cross-sectionally, longitudinally and cross-culturally.

- Methodologically, official statistics (e.g. population census, household surveys) are thought to be an unobtrusive form of method since the participants are not influenced by the knowledge that they are being studied.

With the increasing amount and diversity of information available in the public domain, using existing data may appear to be an easy option compared to collecting primary data. However, there are issues to be considered in terms of practicality and data quality:

- Accessibility of datasets – often access is restricted and bona fides for researchers can be time consuming for the independent researcher

- Lack of familiarity with the data

- Lack of control over data quality, e.g. incompleteness, inaccuracy, sampling errors, etc.

- Incompatibility between datasets in terms of timelines, populations, boundaries

- Absence of your key variables (Bryman, 2012).

Quantitative research of a descriptive nature

Quantitative research takes two distinct forms: research which is of a descriptive nature, and research which investigates cause and effect. We will now explore some of the issues involved in descriptive quantitative research, which requires us to pay attention to a number of key areas.

1. The research question

As we have established in Chapters 2 and 3, it is important to remember that the research question drives the research in its entirety. Everything else flows from the research question.

2. The sample

In a descriptive study we need to pay close attention to the sample we use. In a perfect world we would be able to draw on everyone in the world. We would not miss anyone out and would, therefore, be able to make statements about our study with ease. However, we are obviously unable to do this. As a consequence we must draw on a smaller sample, and design our study so that this sample either accurately or reasonably represents everyone else.

As our data must be gathered in such a way that we can confidently use it to describe the attitudes and opinions of the entire population, our sample should allow us to demonstrate what is causing the effect we are studying. This means that we must gather our data carefully and systematically.

We must ensure that the group of people, or the situation, sampled does not create any variables which may be deemed to have caused the effect instead, or which bias the sample in any way; for example, using only males in our study and then attempting to explain the opinions of both men and women.

We must consider the problems of:

a) the sample being representative of the population, or being truly random

b) bias in the sampling procedure which may influence the results

In order to fully explain the principles of sampling, a separate section is presented further on.

3. Analysis of results

Within quantitative research, results can be analysed using descriptive and inferential statistics – or a combination of both. Quantitative research that is largely descriptive in nature will mainly use descriptive statistics. Quantitative research that is scientific in nature will almost certainly use a range of inferential statistical measures. Please see Chapter 8 for an overview of key issues to be considered in relation to both quantitative, and also qualitative, data analysis.

Scientific quantitative research

Scientific quantitative research involves the testing of a research question in order to ascertain if there exists a cause and effect relationship between the variables. There are three things we must consider.

1. The control of variables

There are four types of variables we must take into account.

I. **The Independent variable**: the variable which we are investigating and hope to demonstrate causes or influences the outcomes.

II. **The Dependent variables**: the variable which is (hopefully) changed by the Independent variable. It is said to 'depend' on the independent variable, hence its name.

III. **Extraneous/Intervening/Mediating variables**: these variables mediate the effects of the Independent variable and may interfere, and not allow us to make a cause and effect connection between the Independent Variable and the Dependent Variable. They may be an alternative explanation for our findings. For example, the number of chick ospreys successfully hatched (dependent variable) is a direct product of the health (among other factors) of parent ospreys (independent variable). However, this can be affected by the availability of food during the same year (a mediating variable).

IV. **Confounding variable:** These variables are a type of extraneous variable which change with the study and therefore may also offer an alternative explanation of the findings.

2. The hypothesis

Once you have managed to develop a research question, that's the first hurdle overcome. If you want to examine a relationship between two (or more) variables, and particularly if you are hoping to establish a cause-effect relationship, you will now most likely want to focus your question further by developing a hypothesis. Not all studies have hypotheses. Descriptive qualitative studies in particular tend not to use them. However, hypotheses are a fundamental scientific tool in contexts where research questions need to be turned into a testable statement or a set of testable statements in order for them to be operationalised – or quite simply, investigated.

To determine a hypothesis, we work out what 'variables' we are exploring and build a test to find out more about them. A testable statement is of course otherwise known as a 'hypothesis'.

What we think of as our 'hypothesis' is actually known as the 'alternative hypothesis' because it suggests that the results happened because of a variable systematically influencing the results and not simply as the result of chance. Therefore, it is really an 'alternative explanation'. However, in a statistical test we don't actually test this hypothesis. Instead, we test what is known as the Null Hypothesis – a statement which takes into account all other possible outcomes and in particular the possibility that the results are simply a chance occurrence.

If we can reject the Null Hypothesis, then by definition our 'alternative hypothesis' may be a good explanation of the effect. Because we are using tests based on probability we can never say we have proven the effect. As an example, in our report we would use a shorthand expression:

Alternative hypothesis – H1

Null hypothesis – H0

The Alternative Hypothesis is a testable statement made by the researcher at the start of a quantitative study. It is derived from the research question and tests a

51

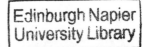

specific, or discrete, aspect of it. It is a statement which is made up of very specific variables and a prediction of the effect which is expected. It does not contain any extra information or details. Instead it contains only:

> The Independent Variable (IV)
>
> The Dependent Variable (DV)
>
> The Prediction of change (P)

Therefore, it states:

- the Independent Variable (IV) we are testing the effect of

- the Dependent Variable (which we are measuring the impact of the IV on)

- the Prediction of the effect the independent variable will have, which will be described by a verb or a short phrase such as, 'increases', 'decreases', 'will improve', etc.

An example of a highly simplistic hypothesis would be: 'Fertiliser increases plant growth'.

In this basic hypothesis:

- IV = The variable of 'fertiliser'
- DV = The variable of plant growth (which can be measured)
- P = The predicted effect, which 'increases'

The more clearly we state the hypothesis then the more robust, valid and reliable it will be as a testable statement. In the section on statistical analysis of data we will demonstrate how these two terms – validity and reliability – are put to use.

3. The design and conditions

In experimental research, creating different conditions in a study is something to pay particular attention to. If we are trying to demonstrate a cause and effect relationship then we need to ensure that we do not introduce any other variables by accidentally creating bias through inappropriate conditions. A condition is another word to describe the features of the independent variable we are exploring. In the example of the fertilizer given earlier, we may decide to have three conditions:

- Condition A: No fertilizer given to plants

- Condition B: One scoop of fertilizer given weekly

- Condition C: Two scoops of fertilizer given weekly

We can account here for the impact of each condition on the growth of plants. This allows us to make a statement about the effect of the independent variable on the dependent variable.

When working with human beings we have to consider a variety of things that might include:

- the past experience and skills of the participants
- the age of the participants
- the gender of the participants
- the social class of the participants

- the employment status of the participants

If we were to design a study to test the difference of ability in reading tests between men and women then it would be clear that gender is the independent variable and the scores on the test are the dependent variable. We would therefore have two conditions: men and women.

However, because of the individual differences which may exist (for example in social class, past experience, age, etc.) then we would have to carefully match the participants in order to ensure that one group did not have an advantage over another group.

In order to test cause and effect we need to control the other variables. There are three key forms of design which can be used to ensure that this happens:

Independent groups design. This uses different participants in each condition, and is valuable for studying discrete skills or properties which create separate groups (e.g. gender, difference between young and old people, and difference between national groups).

Repeated measures design. This uses the same participants in both conditions. Therefore, a person may do a task in condition A and then do a different task as part of condition B.

Matched pairs design. This is a special kind of independent groups design where we are able to match participants' abilities and skills very accurately. This gives us an important advantage as we are unable to rule out any other extraneous variable.

Order effects are a key issue in repeated measures designs. If a participant completes condition A and then completes condition B, the order in which they complete the tasks may have an impact on the result: There are two factors we need to consider:

Fatigue: it is possible that a person may become tired after the first condition and therefore the results of the second condition will not properly reflect the ability.

Practice: it is possible that a person may gain experience during the first condition and as a consequence may be better, because of practice, in the second condition. As a result the scores may be influenced by practice and not by their genuine ability.

We can never be sure whether there is a practice or fatigue effect. We can only plan to eliminate order effects but not a specific order effect. In order to control for 'order effects' and ensure that they do not influence the results of the study, we must counterbalance. There are many ways of counterbalancing to control for order effects. Two straightforward ways are:

Option 1.

Participant 1 completes the conditions in the order A then B.

Participant 2 completes the conditions in the order B then A.

They continue this way until all participants have completed the study.

Results will therefore be a combination of participants completing the conditions in both directions but counterbalancing for both fatigue and practice.

Option 2.

A more advanced way is to use the ABBA method. Here participants do all conditions in this order:

A then B, then B again, followed finally by A again.

Sampling

By necessity, through pressures of time, funding and pragmatics, data rarely comes from an entire population. Therefore, we need to try and use a sample of the population which has no inherent bias and which can be said to accurately represent the whole population. This will allow us to generalise any findings from our research on the sample to the whole population.

Essentially the purpose of sampling is to use a relatively small number of cases to find out about a much larger number (Gorard, 2003, p. 57). Therefore, how you sample directly affects the quality of your survey results. An obvious example would be that if your sample is not representative of the larger group you are interested in, you cannot say that the results based on the answers given by your sample group reflect those of the larger group.

Here are some terms you should be familiar with:

- A population is the group you wish to study, e.g. all members of the National Trust.

- A sample is the subsection of the population that you actually study.

- A sampling frame is a complete list of the population being researched.

Ideally, the sampling frame is identical to the population, but typically the sampling frame is a subset of the population. For example, if the population you are interested in was all the ecologists in the UK, your sampling frame could be a list of the ecologists who are members of the Institute of Ecology and Environmental Management (IEEM). However, even though the IEEM has a large number of members, some ecologists are not members of this institute.

Sometimes, a sampling frame may not exist for your population of interest (e.g. a complete list of visitors to the Cairngorms National Park).

Probability sampling

There are two strands in sampling approaches – probability and non-probability sampling.

Probability sampling is particularly relevant to quantitative research, and is concerned with the generalisability of findings. Probability is the likelihood or chance that something would happen, and we can say that probability equals 1 when something is certain to happen. Therefore, the probability of an unbiased coin landing head side up is 0.5. Probability sampling is possible only when:

a) Each person in the population of interest has an equal chance of being part of a sample (i.e. a minimal chance of researcher bias being involved).

b) A sampling frame exists

One of the most important things about probability sampling is that it allows you to draw statistical inference from your sample to a larger group than your sample.

However, even with the sample selected using probability sampling, you should be very careful when making inference. For instance, statistical inference is possible between a sample and a sampling frame, but not between a sample and the population. Statistics will help to extrapolate from sample to sampling frame, but not from the frame to the population. For the latter, you will need non-statistical arguments and justification.

You should also always remember that a sample is not equal to the population.

Types of probability sampling

Types of probability sampling include random sampling, systematic sampling, stratified random sampling, and multi-stage or cluster sampling. We'll now consider these in turn.

Random sampling is an ideal form of probability sampling, because it enhances the representativeness of a sample by keeping sampling error to a minimum and avoiding researcher's bias. Bryman (2012) gives an example of random sampling processes:

I. Define the population: all full-time students at a particular university (5000)

II. Select a sampling frame: a list of full-time students

III. Decide a sample size (500)

IV. Assign all the students in the list of full-time students consecutive numbers, 1 to 5000

V. Select 500 different numbers using a table of random numbers or a random number generator (again, like sample size calculators, there are freely available online).

The key to random sampling is that everyone in the sample frame must have an equal chance of being selected for the sample.

In systematic sampling an interval (the gap between selected cases) known as 'n' is chosen and every nth element of the population is sampled, starting from a first element which is chosen randomly. The main problem with this approach is, however, if the same characteristics recur at every nth point in a population, you end up selecting cases with the same characteristics.

In stratified random sampling the population is divided into subsets according to some characteristic that is considered to be relevant to the research. Then separate samples are drawn from each subset, using random or systematic sampling. This method is based on the principle that there is significantly less variation within each subset than across the whole population as a whole.

Multi-stage or cluster sampling is used when the cases you are interested in occur in natural groups (clusters) such as institutions, districts, schools. So you can redefine the population of interest to be the clusters (institutions) themselves and then select samples from them using one of the other probability sampling methods. Cluster sampling is handy when the population of your interest is widely dispersed because it reduces your travel (from Bryman, 2004, pp. 90-2).

Sample size

Now you may wonder about the size of our sample and how we know if it is large enough.

One approach is to 'Have a sample as large as you can manage'. However, it is possible to define a sample size which will be efficient for your study. A number of online sample size calculators are available to help you do this. They require you to specify a number of key elements including:

a) Confidence limits. This is the probability level beyond which you are confident the results have not happened by chance. This is based on the 5% figure we looked at earlier.

b) Confidence interval. This is the margin of error in your final results as a percentage.

A good online calculator will explain the terms and how to use them. Please see the companion website for links to a number of recommended online sample size calculators.

Where it is possible, a large sample is useful because it helps deal with a number of issues:

Non-response. Some questionnaires will not be returned and some of the returned questionnaires will be unusable. Non-response is also related to representativeness since there may be differences between those who responded and those who did not.

Sampling error. Sampling error can be reduced by having a large sample size.

Sub-groups. When you designate sub-groups through research design or the questions asked, each group should not be too small. For example, when asking about TV ownership, it is likely that only a very small number of the respondents will not own a TV. Thus, to have enough respondents in that category, your sample size needs to be large.

Analysis methods. The sample must be large enough to accomplish what is intended by the analysis. This means that you need to know about analysis methods before administering a survey. For instance, if you plan to use bivariate relationships between a question with two categories (e.g. gender) and a seven- scaled question (e.g. attitudes towards organically produced food), there are potentially fourteen different answers. This means that you should have a reasonable number of responses for each of these fourteen.

The accuracy of the findings. The larger the sample, the more accurate the results are likely to be as an estimate for the population. It is very useful if you can get a statistician to calculate an appropriate sample size for your project. However, in most cases you will have to do it by yourself. One suggested rule to decide sample size is between five and ten times the number of variables used (Gorard, 2003). For instance, if you have six variables (e.g. age, gender, income, educational attainment, place of living, car ownership), you will need a sample size of between thirty
and sixty. When exploring differences between subgroups in a sample, any sub-group should have fifty or more cases (Aldridge & Levine, 2001).

Other points to remember when deciding sample size are:

- Small sample sizes can be justified by the nature of the research.

- A sample does not have to be proportionate to the population, because the accuracy of findings is related to the absolute size of the sample. Therefore, a sample of 100 can be equally good as 1000 for a population of a million.

However, you should always make an effort to get a sample size as large as you can manage in order to increase the representativeness and accuracy of results.

Non-probability sampling

Non-probability sampling is used when probability sampling is unnecessary as well as impossible. This may be the case for research projects and contexts within which, for example:

- you do not intend to collect data on a general population

- a population is so small you have to use whoever/whatever is available, e.g. endangered animals, patients treated with medicine recently invented

- it is difficult to reach the population, e.g. HIV-positive patients, people with criminal records

- you are undertaking a pilot study.

Non-probability sampling methods

Some of the commonly used non-probability sampling methods are:

Purposive sampling: selecting cases on the basis of specific characteristics.

Snowball sampling: which relies on each case to supply details of further cases so that the sample grows steadily in number. This method can be useful when: sampling frames don't exist; cases are rare and/or geographically widely distributed; cases know each other and are willing to supply information about each other.

Quota sampling: used to produce a sample that reflects a population in terms of the relative proportions of people in different categories, such as gender, age groups. It is different from stratified probability sampling because the selection of individuals within the chosen categories does not involve probability sampling.

Convenience sampling: based on a selection of cases which are easily accessible to the researcher, e.g. using students in the researcher's class to develop a research tool.

As you can see from these methods, non-probability sampling is not recommended if you aim to achieve generalisability within your research (that is, the extent to which your research findings can be applied to comparable contexts and with confidence). This is one reason why non-probability sampling is often used in qualitative research. When using non-probability sampling, you need to carefully justify why this approach is appropriate for your research.

One Tailed or Two Tailed Testing

All statistical tests are based on probability. Figure 4 shows a normal distribution curve which is also a probability curve. It describes the way normal events in the world naturally happen.

For example, in mature adults we know that only a few people have very large feet and only a few people have very small feet. The majority have average sized feet. Therefore, we can see in this graph that it has two tails. The tails of the graph narrow down to the baseline. At the left-hand side are low scores, and there are only a few of them; at the right hand edge of the graph are high scores and again, there are only a few of them. We can see in the middle that the graph rises substantially and this represents the majority of people in the sample.

Our hypothesis may predict a particular direction that the dependent variable will change towards. If we state that an independent variable will cause an increase then we would expect the graph to skew towards the right. If we predicted decrease we would expect the graph to skew towards the left. However, sometimes we may not predict a particular direction of change but simply say the independent variable will 'affect' the dependent variable.

Where we predict the direction of change, this is known as one-tailed hypothesis. When we do not predict a specific direction it is known as a two-tailed hypothesis.

When we carry out a statistical test we need to specify if we are using a one-tailed or two-tailed hypothesis as this will have an impact on how the test calculates a result.

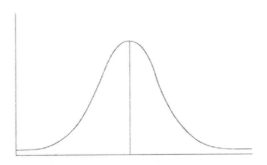

Figure 4: A Normal Distribution Curve

Glossary of terms

At this point it might be useful to explore some key terms in quantitative research which you may be confronted with when delving into a textbook or an online resource.

Conditions are the way that the forms of the Independent Variable are organised. In a simple example we may have an Experimental Condition and a Control Condition. The Experimental Condition has a specific IV which we are testing and the Control Condition provides a normal baseline against which we can measure any change. In a more complex study we may have several conditions of the IV, for example, we may be interested in comparing three or more reading schemes in primary schools. Each scheme would be a condition,

Descriptive statistics allow us to describe the data using basic calculations such as Mean, Mode, Median, Range and Standard Deviation.

Dichotomous (binary) variables: variables with only two categories, e.g. gender (F/M), variables examined through Yes/No questions.

Effect Size is a measure of how effective the probability level we measure through inferential statistics is. We may find that a result is statistically significant but the effect size is low. This adds to our understanding of the relationship between Independent and Dependent Variables.

Indicators are used to explore concepts that are less quantifiable, e.g. ethnicity, job satisfaction.

Inferential Statistics allow us to 'infer' meaning from a set of results. By using statistics we can work out the probability of the results happening by chance. If the probability of chance is low then we consider our Independent Variable to have had the desired influence.

Interval and Ratio variables, known as quantitative (continuous) variables, are real numbers and the numbers have meaning. They have equal intervals between them – 1, 2, 3 – and they have meaning in terms of 'order' and 'magnitude'. The differences between interval and ratio data are subtle.

Nominal variables is another term to describe categorical data – identified by names or labels. There is no inherent order to the categories, e.g. religious affiliation, nationality or profession.

Measures are quantities which refer to things that can be relatively unambiguously counted, e.g. income, age, numbers of insects in a quadrat, reading scores in primary age children, etc.

Ordinal variables: categories can be rank-ordered, but the differences between the categories are not equal across the range, e.g. social class, job position in a hierarchy, agree-disagree answers.

Qualitative (categorical) variables are variables which are not numerical and do not naturally fall into an order or ranking, e.g. the colour of cars, or the names of people. These can be considered as categories. Issues can arise here, however, as the colour of belts in Judo look like categorical variables but they are part of a hierarchy and follow a rank order. Look out for this in your own data.

Ratio (continuous quantitative) variables involve absolute measurement, such as height or age, and these scales have a meaningful, absolute zero point. In other words you cannot have a negative number for your height.

The scale of measurement starts at 'zero' and moves up the way not down.

Reliability refers to the consistency of a measure of a concept; in other words, 'the extent to which a test or procedure produces similar results under constant conditions' (Bell, 2005, p. 117).

Statistical Significance is a result which falls below a threshold level of 0.05 or 0.01 which we can use to infer meaning, or that our results have significance, and a cause and effect relationship between the variables has been established with confidence.

Unit of analysis. The unit of analysis is determined by your approach to data analysis. For example, if you were interested in disease rates in squirrels, your unit of analysis could be individual squirrels in a certain area (a sample of them); or you could be comparing disease rates between UK counties (so the county would be your unit of analysis).

Validity. Within quantitative research a key question of validity is whether the variables in your hypothesis are actually measuring what they are intended to examine. This requires a great deal of thought and should be an integral part of translating a research question into a hypothesis.

Optional Activity

If you propose to use quantitative methods within your research project, think about which of the quantitative methods or approaches we have explored here (and via the resources on the companion website) fit best with your proposed research. Consider your research question or questions, and list the pros and cons for the different quantitative methods you might use.

Background Reading

Bell, J. (2005) Doing your research project: A guide for first time researchers in education, health and social science (4th Edition). Maidenhead, England: Open University Press.

Black, T.R. (1999) Doing quantitative research in the Social Sciences: An Integrated approach to research design, measurement and statistics. London: Sage.

Bryman, A. (2012) Social Research Methods (4th Edition). Oxford: Oxford University Press.

Creswell, J.W. (2009) Research design: Qualitative, quantitative, and mixed methods approaches (3rd Edition). London: Sage.

Gorard, S. (2003) Quantitative methods in socialscience. London: Continuum.

Hakim, C. (1987) Research design: Strategies and choices in the design of social research. London: Allen & Unwin.

May, T. (2001). Social research: Issues, methods and process (3rd Edition) Buckingham: Open University Press.

Robson, C. (2002) Real world research (2nd Edition). Oxford: Blackwell Publishers.

6 QUALITATIVE RESEARCH METHODS

Objectives

In seeking to support a fuller understanding of qualitative research, this chapter aims to offer further insight into different qualitative research strategies and approaches, and to explore interviews and focus groups as key methods of collecting data within qualitative research approaches.

Key Points

Qualitative research, as we established earlier, is a necessarily more subjective and interpretative means of research than quantitative approaches. Indeed this is a key strength of qualitative research which, when undertaken mindfully and with appropriate rigour, can provide us with a rich, in-depth description of phenomena, perceptions, and behaviour within social and cultural contexts.

Areas of application

As explored in Chapter 2, qualitative research tends to be concerned with investigating and attempting to arrive at a better understanding of, or explanation for, behaviours, dialogues, experiences and perceptions in social contexts. When employing qualitative research in such contexts, we are usually interested in what we can observe as a researcher, or what we can understand through the subjective experiences described to us by participants in our research.

Different qualitative research strategies or approaches lend themselves to different data collection methods, and place different emphases on what it is we are researching and why. We will now consider a range of qualitative approaches to research and research design. What follows is not an exhaustive overview, but distinguishes between some of the main approaches you may encounter.

Qualitative research strategies and approaches

There are a range of established and widely practised qualitative research strategies and approaches, including narrative inquiry, phenomenology, ethnography, case study research, grounded theory, and discourse and content analysis. Within each, there are particular issues to consider and methods to be employed. While we provide a basic overview below, there are many good books and articles available to provide further detail on each of these approaches.

Narrative inquiry

Within which participants tell their stories and explain the meaning of these narratives to their lived experience, often through semi-structured interview. Within narrative analysis we might attend to why and for whom a story was constructed, including the cultural discourses drawn upon. We may also apply, as is appropriate, different methods of narrative analysis including structural narrative analysis, performance analysis, and fictionalised representation.

Phenomenology

Phenomenology is concerned with understanding a phenomenon, but rather than considering the phenomenon to be something that exists in the real world as an independent 'thing', phenomenological research seeks to understand the phenomenon from the perspective of the individuals who experience it. The rationale is that the individual's lived experience of the phenomenon is more important than the phenomenon itself. Phenomenology tends to be aimed at finding understandings that can be applied more generally, though in pursuing this the researcher has to 'bracket' (or deliberately put to one side their own knowledge and experiences) in an attempt to capture the essence of the participants' experience through the research process.

Ethnography

Ethnographic research is different from phenomenological approaches because rather than 'bracketing out' the researcher's thoughts and feelings about the subject or phenomena in question, the ethnographic researcher instead attempts to become fully immersed in the subject under investigation as a participant-observer. Ethnography is a research method designed to yield an understanding of an entire culture, for example, an organisational culture. The researcher might spend a great deal of time making field notes and recording observations made, with a focus on constructing a 'thick description' of the culture or sub-culture of interest.

Case study

Case study research involves the study of a case-specific phenomenon. The case itself could be, for example, an individual, a cohort of learners on the same course, a department, or an organisation. Data collection can involve a range of methods appropriate to the case and phenomenon, and case study research may employ both qualitative and descriptive quantitative approaches. It is also important to acknowledge distinction between case study as a research design and method, and case study as identification of a relevant context for study within a research project.

Grounded theory

Grounded theory is a research strategy that tends to be used when little is known about a topic and there is little theoretical explanation for it. Theory is generated through qualitative inquiry (often using semi-structured interviews), and involves iterative analysis of data as soon as it is generated. New data is compared immediately to data already gathered, with data gathering ceasing once 'saturation' (the point where nothing new emerges from the data) is reached.

Discourse and textual analysis

Discourse analysis involves the analysis of language in written, spoken and other forms, while textual analysis involves a range of approaches to analysing the content and conveyed meanings within texts that can include films, advertisements, images, and clothing. Both are broadly concerned with identifying the deeper social meanings – including dominant and competing interpretations – that are inherent in the data they are dealing with.

If you would like to explore any of the qualitative strategies and approaches outlined above in more detail, please note that the companion website for this book links to a range of further resources.

Interviewing and focus groups

As we explored in previous chapters, and as may be evident from the above, qualitative research – and qualitative data – is far more subjective in nature than quantitative research and data. Often taking the form of the words spoken by individuals in their normal social habitats, qualitative data is usually unique to the individual from which it is sourced. In this sense, the data is usually very meaningful and subjective; often described as being 'rich' or 'thick'.

Transcriptions of interviews or the proceedings of focus groups are prime examples of this type of data. In raw form, it is made up of pages of text, or audio or visual recordings. As such it is highly unlikely that two participants will generate the same raw data. Contrast this with quantitative data where individual participants may score exactly the same on a memory test.

Gathering such data very often involves the direct interaction between the researcher and the participant. This can bring its own difficulties in that the researcher may be led into asking questions of the participant that are influenced by the researcher's own preconceptions (see the above description of phenomenology and 'bracketing').

There are several different data gathering methods available to the researcher that involve direct interaction between the researcher and the participant and these are:

- Interviews

- Focus Groups
- Observation
- Questionnaires

We will now briefly explore some of the key considerations in using interviews and focus groups as two of the main means of data collection within qualitative research.

Structured, semi-structured, and unstructured interviews

Interviews can take a range of different forms including structured, semi-structured and unstructured. The main features of structured interviews are that the researcher will ask a series of questions in a specific sequence that should not be deviated from. The questions themselves are very specific and should not be adapted or altered between participants.

Semi-structured interviews (also known as narrative or in-depth interviews) are not based around prescriptive questions, but instead are based upon an 'interview schedule'. This is drawn up in advance of the interview and forms a series of themes or topics to be discussed between the researcher and the interviewee. This allows the researcher flexibility to follow interesting avenues as they are revealed by the participant and also allows the researcher to adapt and develop the interview schedule as necessary.

This is a very flexible approach and one of the most commonly used methods. It is popular because it allows the researcher the freedom to explore interesting issues that might not have been apparent at the outset of the research. It also gives the participant some freedom to describe experiences or situations that they perceive as significant.

The unstructured interview is often used in a clinical setting where, for example, the therapist allows the patient or client to talk about any issues that are significant or important to them. In research settings, this is a little different and it is used as an opportunistic form of data gathering.

For example, the researcher happens to be in a situation with an individual who is happy to speak about issues of mutual interest. Here the researcher gathers data in an unstructured format as they may have little idea of what to expect. Both Creswell (2009) and Green and Thorogood (2004) provide useful further information on conducting interviews, particularly semi-structured interviews.

Focus Groups

Data gathering using focus groups shares some similarities with interviewing, in that a focus group is essentially a group interview. However, there are important differences to consider. Focus groups involve a number of individuals and as such, it is important to realise that the responses of individuals will be influenced by the presence of others.

For example, if a focus group involving employees is taking place, the lack of anonymity may make some individuals less likely to offer controversial opinions if they consider that these opinions may be heard by the employer. Equally, participants may view the focus group as an opportunity to 'vent' frustrations about the work-place.

In terms of how to construct focus groups, in your

further explorations you may want to consider the advantages and disadvantages of homogenous versus heterogeneous focus groups, and optimum focus group size and number. Much as is the case with grounded theory, as described above, there will come a 'saturation' point with focus groups where additional focus groups bring forth no new data. Views on when this point is reached vary, and in practice will vary for different projects, but running focus groups of between five to eight members, up to three or four times, is a good yardstick. For exploring key considerations in a little further detail, Green and Thorogood (2004; pp. 107-121) offer an examination of several sub-types of group interview, including focus groups.

Optional Activity

If you propose to use qualitative methods within your research project, think about which of the qualitative methods or approaches we have explored here (and via the resources on the companion website) fit best with your proposed research. Consider your research question or questions, and list the pros and cons for the different qualitative methods you might use.

Background Reading

Creswell, J.W. (2009) Research design: Qualitative, quantitative, and mixed methods approaches (3rd Edition). London: Sage.

Green, J. and Thorogood, N. (2004). Qualitative methods for health research. London: Sage

7 MIXED METHODS RESEARCH

Objectives

Within this chapter we aim to define and then explore different approaches to mixed methods research, highlighting key strengths and limitations inherent in mixed methods research practice.

Key Points

As the name suggests, mixed methods research involves using a range of different research methods to gather and analyse data to answer a research question. This inevitably means that mixed methods research is a little more complicated than utilising a single method. Effectively, you are conducting two or more distinct data gathering and analysis phases. This is similar to doing two studies rather than one. Think carefully before you embark on research of this nature as it is a step change in complexity. That said, well conducted mixed methods research has the potential to be more robust and reliable than a study that utilises a single method or approach.

Defining mixed methods research

Mixed methods is more than just using two different approaches to data gathering and analysis. Multi-methods research is similar to mixed methods, but might be entirely qualitative.

For example, a researcher may be employing an ethnographic research design to understand the culture within a business organisation. However, the findings from the ethnographic research indicate that something of interest is occurring amongst a group within the culture under investigation and in order to explore that in more depth, the researcher might conduct semi-structured interviews using a phenomenological approach and then follow this up with a focus group. This is all part of the same study but it uses multiple methods.

By contrast, mixed methods involves both inductive and deductive techniques, and qualitative and quantitative methods.

For example, a researcher who is studying the culture of an organisation may choose to begin with a cross-sectional survey and use those results to inform a series of semi-structured interviews, leading to a theory which is then tested deductively using an experimental design. This would be mixed methods.

Designing mixed methods research

Undertaking mixed methods research should be a positive decision chosen because it is the best way to answer the research question. Creswell et al. (2010) note that there are two basic types of mixed methods – fixed and emergent. Fixed mixed methods is where the researcher sets out to use mixed methods as a strategy, but emergent is where the researcher finds that using one approach (qualitative or quantitative) is not enough to answer the research question, so a second method is used to explore the research question further.

There are different types of mixed methods designs and different authors have slightly different terms for them. Often, they are subject or discipline specific. In other words, they have been developed specifically for use in certain disciplines such as educational research. There are many different designs, but the three main ones identified by Creswell (2014) will be considered here.

Convergent parallel mixed methods designs

This design is probably the easiest to understand and the researcher new to mixed methods will probably want to start here. The term 'convergent parallel' suggests that data will be gathered using qualitative and quantitative techniques at the same time (i.e. parallel). Once data gathering has been completed and the data analysed, the results will be compared to see if the results 'agree' and this is where the convergence happens. This design is a fixed design. In other words, the researcher will deliberately use both qualitative and quantitative methods from the outset.

Explanatory sequential mixed methods design

This method used quantitative and then qualitative data gathering phases sequentially. Generally, this approach initially favours quantitative data gathering, followed by qualitative data gathering. The initial quantitative data is usually analysed before the qualitative data is gathered because it informs the way in which decisions are made about the type of, and approach to, quantitative data gathering and analysis. The notion of 'explanation' is important here in that the results from the quantitative phase are explained by the qualitative data. An example might be a researcher gathering experimental data and then going on to gather qualitative data to more fully explain or illuminate the results from the experimental phase. Participants might, for example, score highly on a measure of anxiety but this doesn't tell the researcher anything about the experience of anxiety. The researcher may then opt to gather qualitative data from the participants to explain the findings, and to come to an understanding of what the participants' experiences of anxiety were.

Exploratory sequential mixed methods design

This is effectively the reverse of the previous design. Here, the researcher gathers qualitative data about something and from this develops a theory or hypothesis which is subsequently tested quantitatively. It is important to remember that qualitative data are rarely generalised beyond the sample from which it is gathered. The researcher might use the results from a series of semi-structured interviews to develop a survey. Survey designs, while not testing a hypothesis, can be generalised to a wider study population. If a grounded theory approach is used in the qualitative data gathering phase, the data can be used to generate a theory to then test experimentally.

Triangulating mixed methods and data analysis

An important aspect of mixed methods research is understanding how the data from two rather different research strategies and traditions can brought together. One of the key elements of qualitative data is that it isn't analysed quantitatively. It is tempting to say that a certain proportion of respondents made comments that could be used to support a theme identified by the researcher. This begs the question 'How can the two types of data be combined?' The notion of 'combining' the data is somewhat false. Triangulation is a better way of approaching this problem. Triangulation, in its simplest form, is using one set of data to confirm the results from a second set of data. In other words, it is a process of validation. When using multiple methods (rather than mixed methods – i.e. two or more qualitative approaches or two or more quantitative approaches) triangulation is essentially the cross-validation of results. The same process for qualitative and quantitative methods is now standard, but beyond this the triangulation of qualitative and quantitative data combine to provide an insight beyond that which could be generated by using a qualitative or quantitative approach alone. This is Gestalt: the whole is the sum of more than its constituent parts.

Strengths and weaknesses of mixed methods research

Mixed methods is a complex approach to gathering and analysing data, but this very complexity means that it can be applied to 'ill structured' problems and questions where a single approach would not yield a detailed or insightful enough picture. Being able to understand a problem from multiple perspectives simultaneously brings with it the potential to gain a richer understanding of objective facts, and subjective understandings of those objective facts.

Science and social science occupy a place in an ever more political world, where mixed methods approaches are increasingly able to provide answers to politically driven (note that 'politics' is spelt here with a small 'p') research questions that require a plethora of methods to answer.

Moreover, as human beings we are subjective in nature. We all have our own unique subjective perspective on our relationship with the environment (and with each other), and it is often not enough to simply study the natural world while ignoring our place within it and our effect upon it. Mixed methods provides us with a way to meaningfully investigate the relationship between the subjective and the objective. An example of this might be exploring the effect of man-made environmental degradation. On the one hand we need to understand the effects of degradation on the natural environment but equally, we need to explore the human attitudes and behaviours that contribute to, or exacerbate, that degradation. Mixed methods can help us explore that relationship.

Summary of main strengths of mixed methods approaches

- A research question can be explored using a range of data types. Rich data from qualitative gathering and analysis techniques can be given perspective through the use of quantitative data, and somewhat dehumanising numerical data can be made easier to relate to if 'rich' descriptions from participants are used to illustrate quantitative data.

- The advantages of quantitative and qualitative approaches can be utilised in a single study.

- Using mixed methods allows the researcher to engage in an additional level of validation.

- Mixed methods provides multiple perspectives on a research question, which can facilitate the development of new ideas that would not emerge from using one method in isolation.

- A more complex data gathering and analysis method has the potential to address more complex problems than a single method in isolation.

Summary of main limitations of mixed methods approaches

- Mixed methods research can demand a great deal of time (in comparison to a purely qualitative or quantitative approach) which the novice researcher may not have.

- Developing a rationale for mixed methods involves the integration of sometimes competing theories. This requires a good understanding of research methodology and paradigms.

- Findings from the different elements of data gathering can sometimes conflict with one another, and may require some skilful triangulation to rationalise.

Optional Activity

Regardless of whether or not you are using a mixed methods approach, further consider and justify the selection of the methods you have chosen to utilise in your study, identifying what each of them contributes to the study. You may want to draw up a table or grid to do this, and utilise any notes you made in relation to the related optional activities for Chapters 5 and 6.

Background Reading

Blaxter, L., Hughes, C., and Tight, M. (2010) How to research (4th Edition). The Open University Press.

Bryman, A. (2012) Social research methods (4th Edition) Oxford University Press.

Creswell, J.W. (2009) Research design: Qualitative, quantitative, and mixed methods approaches (3rd Edition). London: Sage.

8 DATA ANALYSIS

Objectives

To highlight and explore fundamental issues, important broader considerations (with respect to quantitative and qualitative forms of data analysis), and the emerging area of visual research.

Key Points

Data analysis is a complex process, regardless of whether we are utilising quantitative or qualitative research approaches or some combination of both. We can distinguish between different forms of both quantitative and qualitative analysis, and it is important that we are able make informed decisions about what is appropriate to our own research questions, strategies and approaches. While it is beyond the scope of this book and chapter to explore all the intricacies to be considered when planning your data analysis, we can highlight some of the fundamentals.

Quantitative data analysis

As we began to explore in Chapter 5, quantitative research can be analysed in two ways:

a)   using descriptive statistics

b)   using inferential statistics

Descriptive statistics

Descriptive statistics are very important. They are often considered by students to be less important than inferential statistics but this is not the case. They are the first stage in data analysis and tell us very useful things about our data. They essentially allow us to 'describe the data'.

This is the first stage in dealing with numerical data. In its most basic form we can calculate Mean (average) scores and the Range of scores. This will allow us to begin to interpret the data. For example, by simply looking at the Mean scores we will get an immediate indication of the direction of change in the data. We might be able to tell immediately if scores are increasing or if scores are decreasing. Although this does not enable us to state the results with 'confidence' it does give us a first stage indication. We are also able to calculate the standard deviation and Range of scores.

For example, we might see that the Mean score in Group A is higher than the Mean score in Group B, but the Standard Deviation (the level of dispersion of a set of data values) for Group B is smaller than the Standard Deviation for Group A. As a consequence we can state that Group A has produced a more dispersed set of scores, but that Group B scores are clustered more tightly around the average.

Scores	Group A	Group B
Mean	75	67
Standard Deviation	12	6

Figure 5: Example of Mean and Standard Deviation

Therefore, we can see in Figure 5 how descriptive statistics begin to build our knowledge about the sample and how it has been affected by the independent variable. In addition to Mean and Standard Deviation, Frequency Counts (the total number of responses received, expressed as n =) provide a useful way to depict the numerical value attributable to a particular item or items (e.g. who said Agree, Neutral or Disagree to a particular question). Frequency counts, with corresponding percentage values, can be usefully presented in tabular or chart form (e.g. bar or pie charts).

Rennie and Smyth (2015) provide further guidance on how you may decide to present descriptive statistics, for example when you communicate findings in your research report or dissertation.

Inferential statistics and significance testing

The next stage in analysing quantitative data is to work out if the difference between one group and another is actually meaningful. We use the term 'statistically significant'.

This may seem an odd term. However, it is important to understand that a difference in scores may seem to be large, and therefore interpreted as being a 'real' difference, but may in the end turn out simply to have been caused by chance result. Inferential statistics allow us to infer significance, in case the results of our study are not caused by chance but are caused by the Independent Variable (you may want to revisit what we covered in Chapter 5 on Dependent and Independent Variables).

However, note that we cannot prove this. We can only infer this. By using statistics, we can have a high degree of confidence that our inference is correct and our results are significant.

Statistical analysis allows us to come up with an answer. This is known as the probability value, or 'p' value. In statistical analysis we use the convention that if the probability of a result happening by chance can be shown to be less than 5 times in 100 (or 5%), then we can be confident that the result is caused by the independent variable. The expression $p < 0.05$ is shorthand for the statement 'the probability of the result happening by chance is less than five times in one hundred'.

There is another commonly used figure – $p < 0.01$ – which indicates that the probability of the result we have recorded having happened by chance was less than 1 in 100. These two figures – 0.05 and 0.01– are the key statistical probability levels used in inferential statistics.

The symbols $<$ and $>$ mean less than and greater than. If a number is at the narrow end of the symbol then it is smaller. If it is on the open (larger side) side then it is greater. For example:

- 1 is less than 2 = $1 < 2$

- 2 is greater than 1 = $2 > 1$

If our results show that $p < 0.05$ then does that indicate that our hypothesis is correct?

Sadly no, because of the importance of falsifiability in

science we can only use this statistic to demonstrate that the null hypothesis can be rejected. We cannot use it to make a statement that the 'alternative hypothesis' has been proven. Because statistics are based on probability there is always the chance that our results have indeed happened by chance. Although that chance may be small (less than 5 times in 100) it still exists. Therefore, there are two possible errors which can be made using inferential statistics to test our hypothesis. These are known as Type I and Type II errors:

- **Type I:** We reject the null hypothesis when it is actually true.

- **Type II:** We fail to reject the null hypothesis when it is actually false.

Statistical tests

In order to analyse data and come to a decision about the null hypothesis and the alternative hypothesis we need to use a statistical test. There are a range of statistical tests available to researchers. Commonly used statistical tests include: T-Test; Chi Square; and ANOVA.

However, there are many more ranging from the very simple to the very complex. Most large scale research projects which are funded by grants employ statisticians as well as researchers in order to ensure that the project is designed properly and analysed in a suitable manner.

Although a properly planned and designed study will 'naturally' be able to be analysed statistically, in practice inexperienced researchers often reach the stage of the statistical test with a dataset which does not really fit any test. This can be very demoralizing.

Fortunately, there are a large number of 'self-help'

textbooks available on statistical tests. These are often associated with a particular discipline. For example, there are many books on statistics for psychology and statistics in business studies. Such books tend to use examples which are contextualized to the discipline. They can therefore be very helpful. They also adopt a step-by-step guide approach to carrying out statistical analysis. As a consequence, they do not require an in-depth understanding of statistics. Instead they take you through the process of finalising your data one step at a time. They will also outline the format you should gather your data in. Making sure your data conforms to a particular format is very important if you wish to carry out statistical testing.

Decision Flow Charts

In order to gain an understanding about which test is appropriate for our data we can use what is known as a decision chart. These are flowcharts which take us through, step-by-step, the key factors we need to know in order to arrive at the appropriate test.

Simply typing into a search engine the term 'statistical test decision chart' (set your browser to search for images) will let you find a huge number of straightforward flowcharts on the Internet. Most textbooks on statistics also have decision charts. These are extremely useful and will enable you to be much more confident in the design of your study. A decision chart will ask you what kind of test you are doing, what kind of variables you are exploring, and how you are using your sample. Based on this you will be able to work out which of the available tests you should apply to your data.

Quantitative analysis software

In addition to discipline specific statistics textbooks, and the ready availability of decision flow charts, the quantitative data analysis process can be greatly aided by the use of appropriate computer software. This may range from using Excel to log quantitative data and run both descriptive and inferential analyses, to using specialist software such as SPSS (Statistical Package for Social Scientists) for the analysis of quantitative survey responses and other quantifiable data.

Qualitative data analysis

The analysis of data, regardless of whether it is quantitative or qualitative, is about obtaining and generating robust information that can be used to answer your research question. The marriage of data gathering and analysis strategies in qualitative research often results in a data gathering method having an explicit data analysis approach. An example of this is Grounded Theory. As we saw in Chapter 6, within a Grounded Theory approach, data gathering is iterative and demands that each semi-structured interview is analysed before the next one is undertaken. The purpose of this is to identify the point at which no new themes are revealed; sometimes referred to as saturation. Data gathering and data analysis are also intrinsically linked within other qualitative approaches.

In considering qualitative data analysis more broadly, Thomas (2006) suggests that there are three key purposes to qualitative data analysis which are summarised as follows:

1. To condense extensive and varied raw text data into a brief, summary format.

2. To establish clear links between the research

objectives and the summary findings derived from the raw data and to ensure that these links are both transparent (able to be demonstrated to others) and defensible (justifiable given the objectives of the research).

3. To develop a model or theory about the underlying structure of experiences or processes that are evident in the text data.

(Thomas, 2006, p.238)

Thomas goes on to present a good summary of different analysis strategies (see Figure 6). This identifies four different general strategies and these are: the General Inductive approach; Grounded Theory; Discourse Analysis; and Phenomenology. These can all be linked to specific data gathering strategies, apart from the General Inductive approach.

	General Inductive Approach	Grounded Theory	Discourse Analysis	Phenomenology
Analytic Strategies and Questions	What are the core meanings evident in the text, relevant to evaluation or research objectives?	To generate or discover theory using open and axial coding, and theoretical sampling	Concerned with talk and texts as social practices and their rhetorical or argumentative organization	Seeks to uncover the meaning that lives within experience and to convey felt understanding in words
Outcome of Analysis	Themes or categories most relevant to research objectives identified	A theory that includes themes or categories	Multiple meanings of language and text identified and described	A description of lived experiences
Presentation of Findings	Description of most important themes	Description of theory that includes core themes	Descriptive account of multiple meanings in text	A coherent story or narrative about the experience

Figure 6: Comparison of qualitative analysis procedures. Adapted from Thomas (2006, p.241)

Green and Thorogood (2004) also identify Grounded Theory within their consideration of qualitative analysis, alongside Thematic Content Analysis and Framework Analysis. The most simple of this three is Thematic Content Analysis. You may hear this referred to as thematic analysis. Simply put, the researcher goes through the raw data (a transcript or recording is basically raw data) and looks for recurring themes.

If several participants report issues with transport to a hospital, for example, then transport may be an emergent theme. It can be tempting to say that x number of participants said one thing and y said another, but it is important to remember that this is qualitative analysis through which themes and issues should be allowed to emerge from the data. To this end, many qualitative analysis approaches advocate an iterative process of transcript analysis that accounts for everything said by all participants, and which only concludes when all data is captured in themes or sub-themes.

Framework Analysis is a five-stage approach to analysing qualitative data. The first stage is familiarisation. As mentioned earlier, it is a good idea to immerse yourself in the data by transcribing interviews (or focus groups) recordings. Once you have done this, you need to begin the process of identification of a thematic framework. Essentially, you will identify key issues, themes and concepts. The process of familiarisation (or immersion) will greatly help here as recurrent themes will begin to become more obvious.

These first two processes are a little 'amorphous' but the third process – indexing – is more structured. This is the systematic identification of recurrent themes and issues by noting in the margins of the transcripts (or by creating nodes and references on transcripts within a qualitative analysis programme) of where these themes occur. The next part of the process is called charting which involves lifting the themes out of the transcript either by literally cutting and pasting them onto a large sheet of paper or noting them and recording them (a process which can also be automated if using an analysis programme). The themes can then be organised into 'clusters' and perhaps re-organised again until a satisfactory chart has been created. The final phase is mapping and interpreting. This is achieved by reference back to the research question and examining whether themes relevant to the question have been identified.

For a good 'how to' text, see Bazeley (2013). This focuses on the practical aspects of qualitative data analysis and is a good guide to have to hand when engaging in qualitative analysis for the first time.

The process of transcription

Once the data gathering is complete, a researcher will usually have a recording of the interview or focus group. This is qualitative data in its rawest form. It is always a good idea to take a few notes during the interview or focus group and these notes can also form an element of the raw data. This raw data is somewhat 'clunky' and difficult to work with so it makes a lot more sense to transcribe the interview and work from the transcripts. However, there is an argument to be made that essential elements of the data, a layer of richness, is lost in transcription; the vocal inflections and pauses are difficult to capture in transcription and the analysis of these subtle vocal tones can reveal interesting information. Not all qualitative analysis approaches advocate attending to anything other than the words spoken, but it is worth noting that pauses and inflections can be important.

The transcription process itself can aid the analysis of the data. Wherever possible and practical, you as the researcher/interviewer/focus group facilitator should transcribe the recordings as this will help you 'immerse' yourself in the data. This can be a time-consuming process: an interview of about an hour will take perhaps four hours to transcribe. It may be longer for a focus group, as there may be more than one participant speaking at the same time which can be challenging to transcribe.

Once the transcription process is complete, you can then begin to analyse the data. However, this will vary depending on the research method employed.

Qualitative analysis software

In the same way that excellent programmes are available to aid quantitative data analysis, we have seen in recent years an increasing number of programmes and applications designed to help manage and undertake the process of qualitative data analysis. Software like NUD*IST in the late 1990s, which has since become NVivo, makes the storage and analysis of large amounts of qualitative data faster, more efficient and more secure as it can be easily backed up and copied. However, like all forms of analysis software, it is essential that the researcher learns how to use tools like NVivo properly. There are lots of good guides to using NVivo available via You Tube, for example, and you will find links to many of these on the companion website.

Presenting qualitative data analysis

As with quantitative findings, qualitative findings need to be reported in a specific way. The most usual format of qualitative results is that of themes. Broad themes 'emerge' from the raw data (transcripts) through initial review, and through further iterative analysis the researcher will usually refine a set of major themes and sub-themes. Sometimes these themes and sub-themes are presented in tabular or graphical form, but whether or not this is the case the end point of the process is a series of related themes and subthemes which are supported by anonymised quotations from participants which illustrate the theme. This is, in effect, evidence for the identification of the theme. It is good practice to have several illustrative quotes to support each theme. Having just one quote might suggest that the theme was identified from a lone voice, rather than something that multiple participants have spoken about. If however you are restricted by the word limit for your research report, you may consider placing further illustrative quotes in an appendix.

There is also the notion of the 'dissenting voice'. The dissenting voice, where it is revealed through the analysis process, is one participant who specifically disagrees with something that the vast majority of other participants have mentioned. It important to report the dissenting voices, if there are any, and explore the meaning of these perspectives. Do not think that reporting dissenting voices detracts from the strength of your themes. Instead it shows a rigorous approach on your part.

A note on numbers. We have indicated that qualitative data should not involve numbers. However, there is a trend in some academic disciplines and journals to report proportions of participants who support a theme. Be careful about doing this and consider the discipline that you are working in or the journal that you are submitting your work to. Speak to your supervisor about this point if you are unsure. In terms of the numbers of quotes needed to support a theme, there is no hard and fast rule here. That said, you need to have a sufficient number of quotes to illustrate that the theme emerged as a strong one.

Commenting on those themes that emerged, but were less strong or dominant, will also help in illustrating the breadth of data and where your key findings lie.

Visual and documentary analysis

It can be argued that the visual approaches to the understanding of people in society have been around for a very long time, beginning with the first ever drawings. However, the idea of a visual approach to the study of society is a very recent development. Over the past few decades social scientists, in disciplines from psychology to geography, and led from the front by anthropology, have begun to realise the power and relevance of visual data in exploring society and social events and phenomena.

Researching using visual methods is quite different to using images, pictures or even graphs as an illustration of text. Instead, visual methods use images, pictures or graphs to gather information which can then be analysed. There are a number of organisations which exist to foster and develop visual research methods. Among these are journals such as Visual Anthropology and Visual Studies, organisations such as the International Visual Sociology Association and even an International Visual Methods Conference. The disciplines of anthropology and sociology have made great strides in everything from participatory photography to the video ethnography, and from children's drawings to the study of comics and graffiti. There is also a developing body of work on analytical frameworks and approaches, as well as a developing literature of excellent 'how-to' manuals and textbooks.

The production of visual data

Photography and filmmaking are two key approaches to the production of visual data and both have a long history in anthropology. Early work involving photography and film by Margaret Mead and Gregory Bateson in the 1930s and 1940s, during their seminal anthropological studies of communities in Bali and Samoa, heralded a new era in anthropological studies.

The practices of visual methods have since developed apace in the last few decades and we now have a number of approaches which can be considered.

Participatory methods

The famous study, Navajo Film Themselves (1966), by anthropologists Sol Worth, John Adair and Richard Chalfen, is an example of community-based participatory photography and film making. This celebrated project involved the passing of cameras from the privileged position of researcher to the participant and asking them to record their lives from their own perspective. Much of the film made during this project is available on YouTube.

Photo-elicitation

This is the use of documentary photography to provoke discussion in interviews. This approach is often associated with the work of John Collier Jr in the 1970s and 1980s who believed that visual materials reveal something of the people who made them. In conjunction with the communities who produced visual artefacts, insight can be gained through photo elicitation.

Covert photography and film making

The taking of photographs and the making of films without the informed consent of the subject in a public space, is an important area of visual research. Work exploring the way in which communities or individuals operate within a social space can be achieved by the gathering of such visual evidence

Children's drawings

It can be difficult to work with children's drawings without being drawn into interpretation which is classically of a therapeutic nature. However, it is possible to work in this area and draw from perspectives in anthropology, sociology and other areas of psychology which focus on the experience of living in a social world.

Using pre-existing materials

There is a large amount of pre-existing visual material. This can be found, at one extreme, in the archives of a local community museum or, at the other extreme, in the image files of CCTV companies or national newspapers. Other public materials appear on YouTube and of course on the various forms of social media. Comics, magazines, graphical representations, etc. can all be incorporated into, or made the focus of, visual research.

Ethics

Visual methods have the same ethical requirements and considerations as any other research approach, as outlined previously in Chapter 4. However, added to this is the concept of copyright and the laws of privacy. Therefore, we must always be aware of the legality of using images made by other people and the need to stay within the laws of the territory we are working in.

Analysis of visual data

It is possible to apply a wide range of analytical approaches to visual evidence. Content analysis provides quantitative data. Early ethnographers saw the camera as a very useful tool for the recording of artefacts and possessions, and of recording what was there at a specific time. More interpretive methods such as semiotics, discourse analysis and thematic analysis are also equally applicable to the interpretation and analysis of visual data. It is now also possible, with software such as NVivo, to link elements of an image or a film to interview transcripts in such a way that both operate as part and parcel of the one analytic frame. You should think of the visual as simply another form of data which can be analysed and interpreted using the huge range of techniques available today to the social scientist, particularly (but not only) if you find yourself working in a visual field.

Disseminating your research

Unsurprisingly, visual research methods lends themselves very well to visual methods of dissemination. Film making is a clear area where this can be achieved with ease. In the making of a film, consideration has to be taken into account of such issues as voice, representation, argument, and of course the clear presentation of findings. However, filmmaking has an aesthetic which is very much influenced by 'discipline'. For example, anthropological filmmaking may differ greatly from sociological filmmaking. That said, the requirements of the discipline in terms of visual dissemination of findings are very much still developing so it is important you have a good sense of how visual research methods are incorporated into your own discipline before dipping your toe into the water.

Optional Activity

Go to the companion website from where you will be able to access sample quantitative and qualitative data sets, and further guidance on how to work with them. Explore a sample data set (quantitative or qualitative, or one of each if you like) and begin to think about how you would analyse the data in question. What is the nature of the data, and what quantitative or qualitative analysis approaches do you think it would be most appropriate to employ?

Background Reading

Bazeley, P. (2013) Qualitative data analysis: Practical strategies. London: Sage.

Glaser, B.G. and Strauss, A.L. (1968) The discovery of grounded theory: Strategies for qualitative research. London: London, Weidenfeld and Nicolson.

Green, J. and Thorogood, N. (2004) Qualitative methods for health research. London: Sage

Green, J., Thorogood, N. and Green, G. (2013) Qualitative methods for health research (Introducing qualitative methods series) (2nd Edition). Los Angeles: Sage.

Rennie, F. and Smyth, K. (2015) How to write a research dissertation: Essential guidance in getting started for undergraduates and postgraduates. eTIPS: University of the Highlands and Islands and Edinburgh Napier University.

Ritchie, J. and Spencer, L. (1994) Qualitative data analysis for applied policy research, In A. Bryman and R.G. Burgess (Eds.) Analysing qualitative data. London:

Routledge, pp. 173-194.

Thomas, D.R. (2006) A general inductive approach for analysing qualitative evaluation data, American Journal of Evaluation, 27(2), pp. 237–246. doi: 10.1177/1098214005283748.

SMYTH, RENNIE, DAVIES, SILLARS & WOOLVIN

9 UNDERSTANDING THE RELEVANCE
OF YOUR RESEARCH

Objectives

The main objective of this short chapter is to help you come to an understanding of the relevance of your research in relation to what you set out to achieve, the strengths and limitations in what your research is able to put forward, and in relation to both existing and possible future research.

Key Points

While we strive for rigour in the research process, and aim for clarity and coherence in how we analyse and present our work and findings, research is an imperfect process that is influenced by a range of factors. This includes how appropriately we have framed our original research question(s); how effective our methods of data collection and analysis prove to be; and also the extent to which we were able to access and obtain the range of data and participation we hoped for at the outset. It is important that we are able to reflect on and acknowledge the above in presenting our research, so that we can articulate its strengths and weaknesses, and identify areas for further exploration..

Identifying strengths and limitations in your work

We would hope that all research has strengths and merits. Certainly, at a minimum level, if you have devised clear and measurable research questions, and designed a research methodology that enables you to collect and analyse data in a way that is appropriate to your questions and topic, you will be assured of at least a sound level of robustness within the research itself. The strength of your research beyond this will then depend for a good part on how you write up and present your work, including the clarity and coherence of your narrative, findings and conclusions.

However, there are two important points to note in relation to identifying and communicating the strengths and limitations of your work.

The first important point is that research rarely goes fully to plan. For practical and logistical reasons you may not collect all the data you set out to obtain, and here the levels of participation by those involved in your research may not have been what you hoped for.. You may also discover, part way through the research process, that there may have been better ways to analyse your data or better questions you would like to have put to your participants. These issues and feelings are not uncommon, and indeed are to be expected to at least some extent. It is certainly the case that your tutor or supervisor will be aware of potential challenges and pitfalls of this kind, as will the academics who are examining or marking your research project.

The second important point is that there are established research conventions and mechanisms that we can use to scrutinise, reflect on and articulate the strengths and limitations of our work. The validity, reliability and generalisability of our research are all fundamental considerations here, and clearly addressing these issues in your final report is critical in presenting your research.

Validity, reliability, generalisability

In very broad terms, validity refers to the extent to which the research methods you have used can be said to have either directly measured or directly related to the research questions you sought to answer, and the phenomena or issues you sought to explore. This is essentially about the alignment within your research between subject and method. For example, and alluding to an example from a previous chapter, if you set out to establish gender differences in opinion on a specific social issue, but your sampling method resulted in gathering data from a largely male group of respondents, then the validity of that research is seriously compromised.

The reliability of the research concerns the extent to which the methods used could produce the same result under the same conditions within the same context. So, one might ask whether an identically constructed sample of male and female respondents, from the same part of the country, would show the same or near identical gender differences of opinion on the same social issue.

Generalisability concerns the extent to which the findings of your research can be applied, or transferred, beyond the specific context within which the research was undertaken. Therefore, utilising the same example as above, you might reflect on the level of confidence with which you think your findings relating to gender differences of opinion on a social issue within a sample of the population in suburban London can be applied to the wider population of the UK.

Bell (2005) and the other readings below provide a good consideration of validity, reliability and generalisability in relation to (primarily) social science based research. Be mindful though that there are different ways of defining, and also measuring, validity, reliability and generalisability within the context of quantitative and qualitative research, with some differences in particular disciplines too. Reflect on the general concepts, and their implications for your research, but also be mindful within your written report to address them in ways appropriate to your research topic and approach.

Constructing conclusions

A note on constructing and articulating conclusions for your research. The general notion of alignment we explored above applies equally to: the various parts of your narrative or argument; the clarity of linkage between your research topic and question; the data collection and analysis methods you have employed; the findings you present; and the conclusions you draw based on these findings.

Your conclusions must be directly informed by, and have a clear evidence base within, your findings. Some of your conclusions may be more substantial and stronger than others, because there is a more substantial weight of evidence behind them. Other conclusions may still be fair and defensible, but based on narrower evidence or findings. Be clear on this when presenting or communicating your research, and particularly in your final written report.

And remember a very important rule – the conclusions section of your report is not the place to bring in additional data, findings or speculation (see Rennie and Smyth, 2015, for more on this).

Identifying further directions

As you approach the conclusion of your research, and perhaps through reflecting on the extent to which you can say your research is valid and reliable, you will undoubtedly become aware of issues and phenomena that would benefit from further research. This could be in the form of an extension to your own research, or it may be that you identify within the course of your research other related areas that you can see remain underexplored within the existing body of literature.

In terms of being transparent about the strengths and relevance of your own research, be clear on where your research has addressed or contributed towards addressing a particular research need. However, be mindful too of evidencing your understanding about the potential for further research. This should certainly include the further refinements to your research you would implement in the future, with the benefit of hindsight, but also identification of further research avenues for the field.

Optional Activity

Write 200 words outlining what you see as strengths and weaknesses of your research as it currently stands (either at an initial stage of planning, or in relation to the data you have collected and analysed thus far). Think in particular about the extent to which your proposed research complements or builds upon previous work in the same area.

Background Reading

Bell, J. (2005) Doing your research project: A guide for first time researchers in education, health and social science (4th Edition). Maidenhead: Open University Press.

Blaxter, L., Hughes, C., and Tight, M. (2010) How to research (4th Edition). The Open University Press.

Bryman, A. (2012) Social research methods (4th Edition) Oxford University Press.

Rennie, F. and Smyth, K. (2015) How to write a research dissertation: Essential guidance in getting started for undergraduates and postgraduates. eTIPS: University of the Highlands and Islands and Edinburgh Napier University.

Ritchie, J. and Lewis, J. (Eds.) (2013) Qualitative research practice: a guide for social science students and researchers. Sage.

10 WRITING UP YOUR RESEARCH

Objectives

The main objective of this concluding chapter is to provide general guidelines and questions for beginning to write up your research. We will explore ways of approaching writing, and present key issues and areas that you will need to cover through the structuring of your writing. We also examine the practicalities of writing and highlight the importance of knowing when to finish writing.

Key Points

Writing up research projects and findings in a clear and defensible way is a daunting task, especially if you are new to doing this and are faced with producing your first substantial research report or dissertation. However it is a skill that can be learned and honed, with established and widely understood principles and conventions that can be harnessed to good effect.

Approaching writing and getting started

There is no right or wrong way to write up your research. With the increasing use of different methods and methodologies, the writing and presenting of your research is a key aspect to the research process. Starting to write can be a daunting process but also very rewarding. The writing up of your research allows you to share your work with other people.

However it is important to remember that to be able to share your work with others you need to write about your research in a clear, readable, interesting and unambiguous way.

It is good practice to maintain a research diary that keeps a systematic record of how your thoughts have developed throughout the research process, making notes on important issues or existing work that is relevant to your research (Bell, 2005). Starting to write early can help to avoid rushing at the end when you need to submit your work. You want to do justice to all the work that you put in to collecting your data by providing a convincing and thoughtful write up (Bryman, 2008). Although you may not be able to write about your findings until you have collected data, it is possible to begin thinking and drafting out your ideas of how to present and justify your research questions and/or objectives. Likewise you can also begin to structure and draft the theoretical and conceptual ideas from the research literature that have informed your research questions (ibid).

People approach writing in different ways. The more you write the more you will find that your style of writing will develop as you go along. Writing is very rarely – if at all – a linear process and it is not just about presenting your results. It is a continuous process that allows your ideas to evolve and crystallise during the course of writing up. You want to persuade your readers that your findings and conclusions are significant (Bryman 2008), and a good structure is a key aspect of the written report.

Structuring your written research project

Writing is a means of contextualising your own work in relation to other academic work and, in some cases, the policy related to your research. Your argument needs to develop incrementally, which is done through providing new details and facts with clear and informed interpretation of your research.

Be mindful too that each research project is unique. The length of each chapter and how you divide information between the different chapters will, to an extent, vary. However, there is a general agreement on the key areas that you will need to cover for your research project whether you're employing quantitative, qualitative or mixed methods. The following is a guideline of common chapters and their sequence within a research project but these should be discussed with your tutor.

- **Title**

The title should be brief and summarise the main theme or focus of the research.

- **Contents**

List the headings and associated page numbers. If you include tables and figures within your report these also need to be listed separately with associated page numbers.

• Abstract

A good abstract should inform the reader about the purpose of the research, the methods, the principal results, major points of discussion and conclusions.

• Introduction

This chapter explains the background to the study and indicates the main focus, research aims and/or objectives of the research. You can use the introduction to outline the context in which the study took place.

• Literature review

Within this chapter you should contextualise your work in relation to relevant research that has already been carried out, and to broader concepts and theory. It is here that you can critically evaluate other work and identify gaps in knowledge that your research seeks to fill.

• Design and Methodology

This should be used to provide information about how you undertook the research, the methods employed and the rationale for employing these methods. You can also use the methodology chapter to provide more detailed information about where you did your research, your sample, or who your participants were and how they were selected. Whether you have used quantitative, qualitative or a mixed methods approach you should also include a discussion on how you analysed your data and why you did it in this way. The methods used may have particular implications on how you evaluated and analysed your data. It is important to be aware of this and the influence it had on how you reached your research findings. When discussing these different aspects of your research design you need to be able to defend the choices that you have made.

• Results and discussion

You may wish to have these as two distinct chapters or write up your analysis more thematically and so include your results and discussion within a number of chapters. You will likely have more data than you have the word count and time to write about in one research report or dissertation. You will therefore need to weigh the relative significance and/or importance of your findings in relation to the research questions you outlined earlier in your research project, and highlight the implications for your work.

• Summary and main conclusions

This chapter should summarise your main findings and make succinct conclusive remarks based on these. It is crucial to be able to draw the different threads and arguments from your previous chapters together to provide informed and relevant conclusions. You can also use this chapter to highlight future research based on the findings of your research.

• References

This should include all of the references cited, in alphabetical order and of the same referencing style. Your department will likely have a specified style that you should use.

• Appendices

The appendices can often be an underutilised section of research projects. It is important to remember that they are not a place to 'dump' data or information that you could not put into the main body of text. Instead, the appendices should be used to supplement what has been discussed and may include: research instruments (e.g. survey questionnaire, interview schedule) or technical data (e.g. letters sent to gatekeepers if you needed to work with an organization, information leaflet and informed consent forms) (Bell, 2005; Robson, 2011).

The practicalities of writing

After you have an idea of how you will structure your research report, and you are ready to begin writing in earnest, there are a few things to consider at the outset to help you progress smoothly.

Formatting and presentation

Institutions will normally provide specific guidelines on how to format your document. These will normally specify page margins, line spacing and text formatting. These will also likely include guidelines on the inclusion of tables, figures (e.g. charts, graphs, photographs, maps) or direct quotations which should be used if applicable to your work.

Ethical considerations and plagiarism

You should produce an honest and truthful account of the research that you have done. You must also keep in mind the ethical considerations that may have influenced your research. If research participants requested and/or you promised that they would be anonymised and the information they provided confidential, then make sure that you have done this in your writing. This may be particularly relevant for those who have done interviews and observation based methods but it is also relevant for everyone who is writing about their research.

Make sure that you appropriately accredit and acknowledge the ideas of others rather than passing them off as your own. This can be assisted by accurate and detailed note taking. In your notes be clear when you have directly quoted from other sources (this should be fully referenced with a page number), your own paraphrasing of an idea (the source of this should be referenced) or your own critiques/thoughts of other work (Bell, 2005, p.243; Robson, 2011).

Length of the report

There are often word limits and keeping to these suggested or required word limits is a key skill. It is highly likely that you will have generated more data and information than the word limit. Selecting key information, points or themes that will best convey your research and answer your research questions is very important.

Remembering your audience

When writing about your research it is crucial to remember your audience. Your writing style will vary depending on who the audience is. Writing an academic report for instance, will be a different writing style than a report written for a government organization or business sector even if you are writing a report based on the same data.

No matter who you are writing for, it is always important to remember that someone will be reading your work. You need to be kind to your reader and manage their expectations. When you are writing, make sure you are making your points and developing your arguments clearly. Using introductions to signpost your reader to what they will be reading in the chapter and then concluding the chapter by summarizing the main themes is good practice and helps you to structure your writing. You do not want your reader to be making assumptions about points you are raising as they may come to a different conclusion to the one that you make later.

Timing, drafts and rewriting

Factoring in time to write your research project is important. Writing will often take you longer than you think and there will be days that you will not be able to write as you intended. There are some key points to remember:

- Allow sufficient time for revision and rewriting.

- Make a habit of writing regularly.

- Try to create an environment where you can be free from distractions (see Robson, 2011, for their 510 for tips on creating the right writing environment).

- Have a break if you find you are not producing good work.

Depending on the length of the report you are writing it may be helpful to negotiate with your tutor or supervisor to read drafts of individual chapters for constructive comments and feedback. Your supervisor is likely to have a number of activities on the go and factoring in time that will allow your supervisor to read and comment on your work and for you to still submit on time will be necessary. You could also ask a fellow course mate or someone you trust if they understand the main arguments you are trying to convey or to look out for typing and grammatical errors.

Finishing the writing

It is equally important and difficult to decide when to stop writing as it is to start writing. It is always possible to keep analysing and researching into your chosen subject and to keep redrafting your work. It is important to accept that you cannot include everything in your final work. You do not want to divert away from the main threads of your writing and risk losing a coherent structure for your report or dissertation. See Bell (2005, p.62) or Bryman (2012, pp.706-7) for practical check lists of questions to ask yourself when preparing your final draft.

Final thoughts

It is good to remember that 'everything that you do from the start of your research will be preparation for the production of the final report' (Bell, 2005, p. 62). Keeping good notes from the beginning of the research process can be invaluable when writing up your work. Writing is an integral part of the research process and allows you to present and share your work with others. You need to be aware of how you are structuring your writing and the style that you are developing.

Remember the reader of your work. They will not know as much as you do about your specific research interest so you need to present your work clearly and coherently. Be confident in your writing but also make sure that you are writing in a balanced and critical way.

Finally, writing can often be a longer process than you imagine. It is important to factor in time to draft and edit your written work as well as creating an environment around you that will help you to write. Visit the companion website for additional resources relating to writing up, and please do complete the optional activity below to put some of the guidelines presented above into practice.

Optional Activity

Write a 250-350 word abstract about your project which outlines the topic, approach and methods. Share this with a colleague or supervisor and ask for their feedback on whether your abstract clearly articulates what your research is about. Once you can do this clearly and concisely in the suggested word count, you are well positioned to clearly describe and communicate your research to others!

Background Reading

Bell, J. (2005) Doing your research project: a guide for first time researchers in education, health and social science (4th Edition). Maidenhead: Open University Press

Bingham, N. (2003) Writing reflexively. In M. Pryke, G. Rose, & S. Whatmore, (Eds.). Using social theory: Thinking through research. London: Sage, pp. 145–162.

Bryman, A. (2012) Social research methods (4th Edition). Oxford: Oxford University Press.

Creswell, J.W. (2009) Research design: Qualitative, quantitative, and mixed methods approaches (3rd Edition). London: Sage.

Murray, R. (2006) How to write a thesis (2nd Edition). Maidenhead, England: Open University Press.

Rennie, F. and Smyth, K. (2015) How to write a research dissertation: Essential guidance in getting started for undergraduates and postgraduates. eTIPS: University of the Highlands and Islands and Edinburgh Napier University.

Robson, C. (2011) Real world research (3rd Edition). Oxford: Blackwell Publishers.

Sayer, A. (1992) Method in social science: A realist approach (2nd Edition). London: Routledge.

SMYTH, RENNIE, DAVIES, SILLARS & WOOLVIN

REFERENCES

Bazeley, P. (2013) Qualitative data analysis: Practical strategies. London: Sage.

Bell, J. (2005) Doing your research project: A guide for first time researchers in education, health and social science (4th Edition). Maidenhead, England: Open University Press.

Bingham, N. (2003) Writing reflexively. In M. Pryke, G. Rose, & S. Whatmore, (Eds.). Using social theory: Thinking through research. London: Sage, pp. 145–162.

Black, T.R. (1999) Doing quantitative research in the Social Sciences: An Integrated approach to research design, measurement and statistics. London: Sage.

Blaxter, L., Hughes, C., and Tight, M. (2010) How to research (4th Edition). The Open University Press.

Blakie N. (2010) Designing social research (2nd Edition). Cambridge: Polity.

Bryman, A. (2012) Social research methods (4th Edition) Oxford University Press.

Creswell, J.W. (2007) Qualitative inquiry and research design (2nd Edition). Sage.

Creswell, J.W. (2009) Research design: Qualitative, quantitative, and mixed methods approaches, 3rd Edition. London: Sage.

Gerrish K. and Lacey A. (2010) The research process in nursing (6th Edition). Oxford: Wiley-Blackwell.

Glaser, B.G. and Strauss, A.L. (1968) The discovery of grounded theory: Strategies for qualitative research. London: London, Weidenfeld and Nicolson.

Gorard, S. (2003) Quantitative methods in social science. London: Continuum.

Green, J. and Thorogood, N. (2004). Qualitative methods for health research. London: Sage

Green, J., Thorogood, N. and Green, G. (2013) Qualitative methods for health research (Introducing qualitative methods series) (2nd Edition). Los Angeles: Sage.

Guba, E.G. (1990) The alternative paradigm dialogue. In E.G. Guba (Ed.) The paradigm dialogue. California: Sage, pp. 17-30.

Hakim, C. (1987) Research design: Strategies and choices in the design of social research. London: Allen & Unwin.

Hycner, R. H. (1999). Some guidelines for the phenomenological analysis of interview data. In A. Bryman & R. G. Burgess (Eds.) Qualitative research (Vol. 3). London: Sage, pp. 143-164.

Kuhn, T.S. (1962) The structure of scientific revolutions. Chicago: University of Chicago Press.

Manzo, L.C. and Brightbill, N. (2007) Towards a participatory ethics. In S. Kindon, R. Pain, & M. Kesby, (Eds.) Participatory action research approaches and methods: Connecting people, participation and place. London: Routledge, pp. 33–40.

Marshall, C. and Rossman, G.B. (1999) Designing qualitative research (3rd Edition). Sage.

May, T. (2001). Social research: Issues, methods and process (3rd Edition) Buckingham: Open University Press.

Murray, R. (2002) How to write a thesis. Open University Press.

Rennie, F. and Smyth, K. (2015) How to write a research dissertation: Essential guidance in getting started for undergraduates and postgraduates. eTIPS: University of the Highlands and Islands and Edinburgh Napier University.

Ritchie, J. and Lewis, J. (Eds.) (2013) Qualitative research practice: A guide for social science students and researchers. Sage.

Ritchie, J. and Spencer, L. (1994) Qualitative data analysis for applied policy research, In A. Bryman and R.G. Burgess (Eds.) Analysing qualitative data. London: Routledge, pp. 173-194.

Robson, C. (2002) Real world research (2nd Edition). Oxford: Blackwell Publishers.

Robson, C. (2011) Real world research (3rd Edition). Oxford: Blackwell Publishers.

Sayer, A. (1992) Method in social science: A realist approach (2nd Edition). London: Routledge.

Thomas, D.R. (2006) A general inductive approach for analysing qualitative evaluation data, American Journal of Evaluation, 27(2), pp. 237–246. doi: 10.1177/1098214005283748.

SMYTH, RENNIE, DAVIES, SILLARS & WOOLVIN

LIST OF FIGURES

CPSIA information can be obtained
at www.ICGtesting.com
Printed in the USA
LVOW10s1839020317
525948LV00011B/538/P